SEASONS OF A STORIED LIFE

SIXTY-SIX STORIES OF WISDOM AND GROWTH

BY

WAYNE E. SMITH

ISBN: 979-8-328843-20-1

Table of Contents

DEDICATION

I dedicate this book to my late wife, Debra, with whom I spent over forty cherished years of my life but who lost her brave battle to survive in 2021 even though she was 18 years my junior. Debra stuck with me through the good and bad days with never a hint of abandonment. Because of her, I am a better man, and for that, I am thankful. Even though Debra is no longer with me here on earth, she remains permanently in my loving memory.

I also dedicate this book to the memories of two of my children whose lives were cut short way too soon – my daughter, Deborah Lynn, and my son, Michael Wayne. They both were beautiful human beings, and their departure from my life left two painful, irreparable tears in my heart. Rest in peace, my children.

ACKNOWLEDGMENTS

There are many whom I would like to thank for their support throughout my life, but if I attempted to list them here, I would inadvertently omit some and then have to live with the regret of doing so. Therefore, allow me to issue a blanket "thank you" to all who have played a part, however large or small, in my adventurous "where do I go from here" life. That being said, I want to thank my son Roger, my daughter Mya, and my first wife Judy for putting up with me before I learned how to fulfill the role of husband and father properly. There are two people to whom I owe an extraordinary abundance of gratitude – my late wife, Debra, and my youngest son, Justin.

I thank Justin for believing in me and encouraging me to always "think and live young" and accept new challenges. It is he who set me back on a path to higher education at the age of 74, which earned me a master's degree, and now, after finishing my doctoral classes, I find myself embroiled in the arduous task of completing my dissertation. I thank my wife Debra for her unwavering love for me and her "stand with me" support during not only those "easy to take" good times but also the very "hard to stick it out" trying times. She has stepped up in many ways and has proven that she meant it when she took the vow for "better or worse." And it is she who finally convinced me that I should write this book.

SHARE LIFE'S LESSONS

"There is something uniquely beautiful about a person who grows from their struggles and uses the lessons from their experiences to spread wisdom. It doesn't matter what you've done or how far you fell. Be the example that shows others they can overcome that mountain too."

— Shannon L. Alder

PREFACE

We, individuals blessed with a long life, experience three different seasons of life, and within each of those seasons, there are stories to be remembered, as well as what we learned from them. *The Morning Season* of our life is from childhood until we finish our education. After the Morning Season, we experience *The Afternoon Season* of our life, starting with the time we embark upon a career until we retire. The final Season, Evening, commences upon our retirement and lasts until we are beckoned to make our final curtain call.

I have compiled this book with a collection of the stories of my life as they relate to these three seasons: The morning season of my young life, the afternoon season of my mid-life, and the evening season of my senior life. I invite you to take the journey with me as I explore and relate the short stories of the *"Seasons of a Storied Life."* More importantly, I hope you go away with a better understanding of how these "little stories" of our life each provide an opportunity to learn something and become the total of the "complete story" of our life.

FOREWORD

As an educator, it's often the case that you learn more from your students than you could ever begin to teach them. And some are simply unforgettable. Both are true with Wayne Smith.

Wayne arrived in my classroom over a decade ago. There, to take a Professional Speaking course as part of his Master's Program, he quickly became a leader. A natural storyteller who exudes kindness, wisdom, and a depth that invariably developed across the seasons of his life, Smith readily shares his gifts. And at 74, as he embarked on his graduate work, the other students relished his humble, creative, and nurturing spirit. We all were impressed by his decorated life of service and accomplishments and were ever so grateful for his powerful presence that left an indelible mark.

Seasons of a Storied Life is an imaginative, beautiful compilation of poignant experiences that showcases Smith's uncanny gift of unpacking complexity with great accessibility. Wayne is admirable in his endeavors and in revealing his journey so that we may appreciate the triumphs of the human spirit and reflect on our own stories and legacy.

Just as he intentionally contributed within my classroom, Smith's revelations bring us to a greater resolve to appreciate our capacity to weather and maneuver life seasons, all while drawing deep meaning and purpose.

Wayne is a testament to resilience and a true artist. He has contributed significantly to the world, and this book proves the power of story as a catalyst for deep connection.

May *Seasons of a Storied Life* become the impetus for deep reflection and inspiration as you examine the nuances of your own story and recognize the tremendous power of sharing it.

—Kristen Lee, EdD, LICSW

September 2023

"The Morning Season of a Storied Life."

"In childhood, we press our nose to the pane, looking out. In memories of childhood, we press our nose to the pane, looking in."

— Robert Brault

I begin with some short stories of the morning season of my life, from early childhood through my graduation from Mizzou.

A BIRTHDAY PARTY FROM HELL!

Before I begin this story, allow me to note that even though it happened over three-quarters of a century ago, it is still a powerful and painful memory for me. I was four years old, and it occurred shortly after my parent's separation and divorce. For reasons I had never known and not the norm then, I remained with my father while my mother exited my life. I had complete amnesia in my life before my parents split, and I suspect this resulted from the traumatic effect their divorce had on me. At the time of the birthday party I wrote about, I lived with my father in a rented room in another family's home in my hometown, Rich Hill, Missouri.

I have no recall whose party it was. However, I suspect it was one of my father's acquaintances' children. I begged my father not to make me go to the party, but he insisted. I am sure he felt it would be good for me to socialize with other children at the time instead of being isolated from the world outside our rented room. Realizing my anxiety about having to attend the party, my dad capitulated. He agreed to my request that he remain in the car parked outside the house where the party was being held after dropping me off at the party.

He kept his promise; all I remember about the party was that I would go to a window every five minutes, push back the curtains, and make sure he was still sitting in the car. Of course, at the time, I had no idea why I felt the way I did. Why wouldn't a four-year-old want to attend a birthday party and have fun playing with other children? As I became an adult and understood some of the psychological effects divorce can have on a child, I realized that I was fearful of being abandoned by my father. After all, my mother had left me…so how could I be sure my father would not do the same?

I now understand that the damage caused by parental abandonment can be particularly devastating if it happens before the child understands that he or she is not to be responsible for others' actions. If this happens, a child will often grow up believing that something wrong with them makes them unlovable. While the remaining parent may be able to provide emotional support and help the child develop a sense of self-esteem, young children often will still believe they are at fault.

I also have become aware that my parents split and my mother's departure from my life at such an early age had other debilitating effects on my psychological well-being, which extended into adulthood. Abandonment experiences and boundary violations can become an indictment of a child's innate goodness and value. The wounds often strike deep in young hearts and minds, and the genuine pain lingers for years. After many hours on the therapy couch, I finally achieved a sense of self-worth and inner contentment that enabled me to enjoy life. A life where I have come to understand and appreciate the practical value of love and, as a result, also possess the ability to express love, especially for myself, genuinely.

I enjoyed many good times while growing up. However, this dreadful "birthday" event is my most vivid memory, and I have reflected upon it numerous times.

LESSON LEARNED

As adults, we need to be acutely aware that our actions can, and often do, have lasting effects on our children's emotional health. Additionally, I have come to understand why we are more prone to remember bad events in our lives than the good times: negative memories are more likely to be recognized over positive ones because adverse events pose a chance of "danger."

THE LITTLE TIE CLIP OF LOVE

Something happened when I was about four years old that left a lifelong lasting impression on me. It occurred shortly after my mother and dad divorced, and I remained with my dad. We lived in a rented room in another family's home. One day, as my dad dressed to go out, I looked admiringly at the tie clip he wore whenever he dressed up.

It was a simple tie clip made of silver and ceramic that pictured the face of a little black and white dog. Nothing exceptional or valuable, but that made no difference to me. It was something my dad liked. I looked up to my dad as someone I wanted to be like when I grew up. If I had a tie clip like my Daddy's, I would be a mini-daddy and feel much closer to him. So I asked my dad if he would get me a tie clip like his. He said, "Here, son, take mine."

"No, Daddy, I don't want yours. I want one just like yours." Dad then assured me he would look for one.

A couple of weeks passed, and I checked with my dad every other day to see if he had found my tie clip. Then, one day, he came home from work and asked me to open his lunch bucket to get something for him. After clicking open the bucket, I could not believe my eyes. There, nestled beautifully in some napkins, was a tie clip. My tie clip. One just like my Daddy's.

I excitedly held the tie clip tight and even gave it a loving hug. I then ran to where we slept and carefully placed my tie clip in the top drawer of a stand beside our bed. I repeatedly opened the drawer for the next few weeks to ensure my tie clip remained.

But one day, as my dad and I were getting dressed to visit one of his friends for a birthday party, I noticed something strange. My dad wasn't wearing his tie clip. "Daddy, why aren't you wearing your tie clip?" I asked. Daddy looked sad and replied, "I lost it, but that's okay." I thought for a moment. I, too, felt sad. "Here,

Daddy, you can have mine. I don't want you to feel sad about losing yours." At first, my Daddy said, "No, son, you keep it." However, I insisted he take it until he finally gave in, said "Okay," and accepted my offer.

After that, I never saw my dad get dressed up without always making sure that little tie clip was proudly displayed. He often would point to it and say to a friend, "Hey, Joe, look at this wonderful gift my son gave me." That made me feel even better than if I were wearing the tie clip.

I requested one special possession when my dad died a little over two decades ago at 89. You are right; it was that little tie clip. I now wear no other tie clip. I wear one just like my Daddy's. No, that isn't correct. I wear only my Daddy's.

LESSON LEARNED

I learned an important lesson about the true meaning of giving. It is not about getting something but giving and making someone else feel happy and loved. From that day forward, I understood that giving is more important than receiving. To this day, as a senior nearing the age of ninety, I am on the lookout for ways to give, if nothing more than a welcoming smile and wishing someone a good day. It can make others feel good. As a result, I, too, feel good.

Not Only A New Mother But A New Brother, Too

In 2015, at the age of 95, my adopted mother (I prefer the word "adopted" to "step") came to the end of her life here on earth. The nineteen-year-old woman who came into my life in 1939 when I was four and immediately became my adopted mother lived a long life of love and giving. Not only had I received a new mother, but I also now had a new baby brother. He was just a year old when she and my dad married. At the time, my dad and I were bachelors, living in a rented room with another family. But now we had our own family. Not long after that, we moved to the outskirts of our small town in rural Missouri, and then, about a year later, we moved to a farm where I spent my growing-up years.

My adopted mother spent many unselfish hours teaching me the things a mother knows her children need to know. Years after I became an adult, we reminisced about how she helped me learn many things, including how I discovered my A-B-Cs at age five, with her help, while I walked around in circles in the yard. However, among the many things she taught me, one lesson has benefited me throughout my life. In addition to her many other talents, which included crafts and cake decorating, my mother was an accomplished pianist and loved music. As a result, she taught my brother and me to sing to her accompaniment at a very early age and had us perform often at the church we attended.

Because of this, performing in public, I overcame any reluctance I might have had to get up in front of an audience and speak or sing. In high school, I sang in the choir and participated in public speaking. I obtained a degree in speech and drama at the University of Missouri. And it all started many years earlier, standing beside my mother at the piano, singing with my brother.

I have called upon the confidence my adopted mother instilled in me by having me perform in public throughout my life. What she taught me in those early years has served me just as much, or even more, than anything I ever learned in school.

LESSON LEARNED

There are two lessons to be learned in this story. A parent need not be biological to love and rear a child. There is much to be discovered which will serve us well throughout life that is learned outside the classroom.

TRAPPED IN THE OUTHOUSE

This story occurred when I was about six years old, as my memory serves me. And I consider myself lucky to be alive and able to tell it. Well, maybe that is stretching the truth a bit, but back then, I thought I was a 'goner' as I faced the wrath of a wild rooster. I was living with my family on our farm in southwestern Missouri. The year would have been about 1941. Like many others in our neighborhood, we did not have indoor plumbing and no indoor bathroom. Instead, we 'did our duty' in an outhouse. Other names for this little structure-of-necessity were Crapper or Privy. Ours was a three-holer, two big and one small in between. I don't remember sharing my privy-privacy moments with anyone else, even as a young boy. Most had a cutout in the shape of a moon in the door. Ours did not. However, a crack between the boards on the door enabled you to see outside while seated inside.

Our outhouse was about twenty or thirty yards from the house and next to a barn where chickens roamed the grounds without restraint. I am not sure how many chickens we had at the time, but I do remember that among the others was a big rooster who seemed to have it out for me anytime he caught me alone. Anyone unfamiliar with roosters may not know they have spurs with which they can strike and slash, leaving open, bleeding wounds. These are what roosters in cockfights use to conquer and kill opponent roosters. It is like they have a sword or saber to use in mortal combat. No kidding, a raging rooster can be pretty dangerous.

I went to the outhouse this afternoon to take care of business. After I had finished and pulled up my overalls, I started to open the door to the outhouse, but there, standing directly in my path, was this monstrous bird, the big, bad rooster. He was just daring me to step a foot outside the door. He was, in my opinion, ready to attack. I immediately retreated to the safety of the interior and started yelling for my mother or dad to come to save me. After what seemed like an eternity, finally, they both stepped outside the house to see what was so severe that I would be yelling for help.

14

They just laughed after visually surveying the situation and realizing what was happening. What? I am about to be killed, and you are laughing. This isn't the way things are supposed to happen. One of you, at least, needs to rush over and help me get to safety without being murdered.

I was devastated. My mother and dad were going to let me either sit in the outhouse overnight without dinner, or they would allow the rooster, who seemed to grow bigger as each lengthy moment passed, to rip me to shreds with those nasty spurs of his. And there he was, prancing back and forth in front of the outhouse door, daring me to come out and face the music. No way. I was trapped, and those who I thought would come to my rescue were, instead, laughing hysterically at my dilemma. Come on, do something. I am in dire straits here and need your help. After just a few minutes, but what seemed like hours to me, my dad finally came forward and shooed the bad rooster away with the simple stomp of his foot. He opened the door, took me by the hand, and walked to the house. Whew! I am alive and well, after all. Of course, at the time, I, being as young as I was, saw things from a much different perspective than my parents. In my mind, I was in a life-or-death situation, but all they saw was a humorous event where a rooster had somehow decided to call for a duel with a six-year-old boy. In their eyes, it wasn't serious. In my eyes, the rooster may as well have been a six-foot-tall bear ready to devour me for his lunch.

LESSON LEARNED

As parents, we often do not comprehend our children's perspective, and what seems trivial to us can often be traumatic for them. Sadly, this inability to see things from a child's eye sometimes leaves long-lasting harmful effects.

Note: I am pleased to report that I suffered no long-lasting emotional scars due to this incident. Ironically, looking back on it from the perspective of my present age, I, too, find it humorous.

A RING, POPCORN, AND MUD

As I recall, this story occurred when I was about 8 or 9 years old and lived on the farm where I grew up in Southwestern Missouri. We grew corn, soybeans, and wheat in the fields and lots of vegetables in our garden, including a small patch of popcorn, which we mostly savored as a hot, buttered treat for ourselves during long winter nights while listening to programs like 'The Shadow' or 'Fibber McGee & Molly' on our battery operated radio. Sometimes, when we had more than needed, we would sell some of the popcorn to our neighbors, the Green family.

This particular year, we had a bumper crop of popcorn, so my dad made a deal to sell some to the Greens and promised me the money to shell and deliver the popcorn. After shelling the kernels off the cobs, I had about a pound for which I was going to collect a shining quarter. Dad pulled a small paper sack from the cupboard and filled it with popcorn. Handing it to me to deliver the quarter-mile down the dirt road between our and the Green's houses, he instructed me to be careful and not to drop the bag. I assured him I would be meticulous and headed down the driveway to the road, dreaming about what I would buy with the quarter.

Well, as you may have heard, the best-laid plans of mice and men don't always work out. About halfway to the Green residence, I dropped the bag, which hit the dirt and gravel road with a thud. And then it exploded, peppering popcorn kernels all over, mingled with many pebbles. I was devastated. What had Dad told me…"don't drop it." My first reaction was panic. Then, I came up with a plan of action. I will gather up as many of the kernels that I can and stuff them back in the ripped paper sack as best I can, and then dig some mud from the ditch beside the road and plaster it on the kernels that remained on the road so, if my dad (or anyone else) came this way, they wouldn't notice anything unusual or out of place. At the time, I was wearing a signet ring that my biological mother had given me, and somehow, it slipped off my finger without my notice as I dipped my hands in the mud.

With much difficulty, I got about three-fourths of the popcorn kernels back in the damaged and crumpled paper sack, along with a few unwanted small pebbles from the dirt road. Exerting the care I should have used before the tragedy, I arrived at the Green's house and delivered my damaged goods. Being the polite man he was, Mr. Green accepted the popcorn with no mention of its sad state and promptly gave the payment of one quarter.

It was only then, on my way back home, that I noticed my signet ring was missing. I hurriedly returned to the crime scene and, after spending more time than I could explain, I finally had to give up without finding the ring and return home without it. The threat of panic reared its ugly head again. How do I explain the absence of the ring that I had so admired and valued? I don't have the answer and will just have to wait until I am put on the spot before coming up with a "manufactured" tall tale. I returned several times to the place where I had dug mud from the ditch during the next few days in hopes of finding the ring. No success.

In the ensuing weeks, my parents asked me a few times about my ring and why I wasn't wearing it. Repeatedly, I avoided the truth and reported that I didn't know where the ring was. I couldn't tell the truth without admitting that I had dropped the popcorn and spilled it all over the road. As time passed, there were no more questions about the ring, and life went on as usual. However, the fact that I lied has never been forgotten. Instead, it lurks as a haunting memory of my dishonesty. To my knowledge, that is the only time I lied to my parents, and now, more than three-quarters of a century later, I am still uneasy about my decision not to tell the truth.

LESSON LEARNED

Even though it may not always be the easiest thing to do, telling the truth is the BEST option.

WHY? I AM JUST AN INNOCENT LITTLE CREATURE DOING NO HARM!

Growing up on a farm in a timber-laden rural area of southwestern Missouri, the killing of animals was something I witnessed from a very young age. It was simply accepted as a fact of rural life in the mid-twentieth century. The killing was of domestic animals for staple foods and wild animals for the inbred sport of the event.

The domestic animals on our farm that were slaughtered regularly included chickens, hogs, and yearling calves.

When I grew up in the 1940s and 50s, there were no large wild animals such as deer, bears, or even wild turkeys in our part of the country. Coyotes and wolves were the only larger wild animals, and they were plentiful. Smaller wild animals included skunks, raccoons, opossums, rabbits, and squirrels that roamed the fields and timberland. Their numbers, too, were in abundance.

From the time I can remember, a .22 caliber pump rifle and a multi-shell 12-gauge shotgun were prominently open-stored in a wall rack in the enclosed mud room of our house. They were loaded and ready for quick access at any time of need or opportunity.

I started practicing shooting with the rifle at about the age of 10 and also handled the shotgun at an age when it would no longer knock me backward with its massive kickback when fired, probably when I was about 12 or 13 years old.

At approximately 14 or 15, I graduated from target practice with firearms to hunting wild game with them. I would hunt rabbits and squirrels with the .22 and ducks with the 12 gauge. Believe it or not, I was allowed to take off alone and tramp through the timberland in search of some wild animal to capture in the crosshairs of my weapon. This I was allowed to do with no adult supervision.

On one such trip when I was probably around 17, I spotted a squirrel in a tree and, being the sharpshooter I considered myself to be, felled the creature with a single shot. The squirrel toppled from the tree branch and fell to the ground below. I walked over to retrieve my prize and discovered I had not killed the squirrel but severely injured it. As I approached closer, the squirrel looked up at me with bewildered wonderment in its eyes, and to this day, decades later, I recall the shame and guilt that engulfed me in that instant. The poor animal penetrated my soul with its sad, helpless gaze as if to ask: "Why did you do that to me? I have done nothing to you to deserve this!"

At this point, I had no alternative but to put the poor little bushy-tailed tree-dweller out of its misery. I picked up the lifeless body and trekked back home in a state of sadness that was overwhelming. Upon arriving home, I put the rifle in its rightful place in the rack and, from that day on, never once again touched either the rifle or the shotgun.

That decisive day forever changed my thoughts regarding life. And I discovered that I desire to preserve it at all times. When we lived in the Boston area a few years ago, our rented apartment, constructed in 1926, offered easy access to mice. I humanely trapped the little critters and turned them loose outside. I often liberated the mice in frigid temperatures during the winter, sometimes with snow on the ground. And it saddened me to see it necessary to release them in hazardous weather conditions.

Today, I will harm no creature, not even an insect, if I can help. For example, I recently discovered two small scorpions in our home in Texas, one rendering a painful sting to one of my fingers. Yet, in both cases, I successfully and humanely trapped the scorpions and released them outside. They have every right to live just as I do.

19

Before I break my arm, patting myself on the back because I celebrate life, I must acknowledge that I have yet to become a vegetarian. However, I am working on it.

LESSON LEARNED

Life, in all forms, is precious and should be recognized with respect and admiration for the miracle of its creation.

GIRLS, GIRLS, AND MORE GIRLS…WHO WOULDN'T WANT TO LEARN TO TYPE?

My high school years were 1949-1953 at Bryant High School in Rich Hill, Missouri, which I claimed as my hometown, even though I lived on a farm 7 miles from the town. It was a different time and era in a rural area of Southwestern Missouri, midway between Kansas City to the north and Joplin to the south along Highway 71.

In addition to the academic courses one was required to take in high school, back in those days, we also took vocational classes—girls took classes in home economics, and boys took shop, where we learned to weld and use wood lathes. Additionally, I enjoyed my role as a member of the boys' choir and acting in high school plays. Here, I was in my element.

While I cannot attest to being an outstanding high school athlete, I was a member of our school track team, participating as a runner in the quarter mile and on the relay team. I also played left halfback on our Rich Hill Tigers football team.

After football season was over in December of my junior year, I, along with a close friend and classmate, Tommy, was destined to spend the remainder of the school year "hanging out" and killing time in study hall for the last two periods of the day. One day shortly after that, Mrs. Opal Heatherly, who taught typing and shorthand, approached Tommy and me and said, "I want you guys to join my typing class, and if you can catch up in two months, I will give you full credit for the class." Once Tommy and I visited the typing class and realized we would be the only two boys in a class surrounded by all girls, our answer was resounding and affirmative: "Yes" we will take you up on the challenge. I am pleased to report that both Tommy and I made it. We did catch up with the rest of the class and received full credit. Little did I realize, at the time, what a critical life-changing experience learning to type would be for me.

In my professional career as a radio newscaster and advertising copywriter, my typing skills have served me exceptionally well throughout the years and even now, over a half-century later, in my higher education endeavors and composing this book.

In reflecting on the decades that I have been typing, I realize that I have graduated from first using a manual Underwood machine to a Smith-Corona version that had an electric keyboard but a manually operated return carriage, to an IBM all-electric Selectric Model, always with that trusty bottle of white-out close at hand. Finally, about twelve years ago, I put my IBM Selectric away in the closet and placed my fingers on the keyboard of a computer. Why didn't I simply get rid of my IBM? Because I wasn't sure I could master the computer compatibility technique and needed the assurance of a backup plan if it didn't work out. I am here today to announce that it has worked out. Returning to a typewriter would be like reverting to the dark ages of professionally written communication.

LESSON LEARNED

There are manual, vocational skills we may learn in life that serve us just as essential as the academic advancements we may achieve. I shudder to think how difficult it would have been to find a career without becoming a proficient typist. Thank you, Mrs. Heatherly.

The Folly Of Youth

Two times in my youth, I purposely did something that could have brought my life to an early end.

The first occurred when I was 17 and still in high school. Gene, a high school friend, and I decided to leave home during the summer and do what was known as "follow the wheat harvest." We packed up and took off for Oklahoma in my truck to where the yearly harvest commenced. We planned then to follow the harvest up through Kansas and the Dakotas. We would help harvest wheat, and I could earn extra by using my truck to deliver the harvested grain to a local elevator, where it would be stored until loaded in train cars for distribution throughout the country.

The first job we landed was working for a wheat Farmer in Enid, Oklahoma, just south of the Kansas border. In addition to receiving payment for our work, we also were given room and board. The room part was two sleeping cots in the barn. It was a good deal for young guys trying to earn extra money.

After about two weeks, the harvest was completed in Enid, and it was time for Gene and me to move onward north, following the harvest as the wheat ripened later in the farther north. However, the wheat farmer we worked for offered us good pay to hang around and plow the empty wheat fields in preparation for the following year's crop. At that time, the accepted practice was to plow the ground and then disc it before planting the seeds. Plowing meant turning the soil over approximately six inches deep. The front wheels of the tractor we used to pull the plow would sit in the six-inch furrow of the last passage and practically guide itself without much steering.

The plow we were pulling would turn over about four feet of soil on each swath across the field. A constant problem was that the left-on-the-ground wheat straw would clog up in the plow and make it necessary to stop and get off the tractor, walk back and remove the straw to keep the plow working correctly. Well, this was a pain in that part of the body we sit on. I decided there was a quicker way to make things work properly. All I had to do was crawl off the tractor, leaving it to drive itself in the furrow, climb back on the plow, and kick the straw out before it became too clogged to work. My ingenious plan worked well, and I continued this practice without considering its danger.

If one of my legs had gotten caught in the plow, leaving me helpless to dislodge myself and return to the tractor, I could have been dragged to death or severely injured. And because the work was done in isolation from anyone else, there would have been no one to rescue me. Thankfully for me, it never happened.

The second time I put myself in potential peril was when I was a college student and working summers for my stepdad on railroad bridge construction. This particular summer, we were working in Joliet, Illinois. I stayed with my mom and stepdad in an apartment near a reasonably large creek.

After a deluge of rainfall one night, the creek overflowed, and the basement of the apartment where we were living became flooded. Our landlord, who lived upstairs, had several items stored in the basement, and, of course, everything ended up quite a muddy mess. The morning after the rain, the landlord told me she would pay me $100 to retrieve anything not ruined from the basement and, after the water receded, clean out the basement, throw away any unsalvageable items, and shovel out the mud.

Without giving it a second thought, I agreed and put on some work clothes to wade into the basement water – nearly chest-high to see if anything could be salvaged. I waded into the water without regard for the possibility that it had risen so high that it also covered the electrical outlets in the basement. If that were the case, I would have been instantly electrocuted. Again, thankfully, it did not happen, and I live to tell the story.

LESSON LEARNED

I learned this lesson later in life. While it is much easier to blame folly rather than stupidity for our actions, there is no difference. Folly means lack of good sense, but stupidity means behavior that shows a lack of good sense or judgment. They are the same thing.

JIM FLEW THROUGH THE AIR LIKE A RAG DOLL!

After graduating from high school in 1953, I moved to Chicago and worked with my stepdad, the crew manager of a construction gang that worked to repair bridges for the GM&O Railroad. I worked as a laborer doing grunt work like breaking concrete with jackhammers, chipping guns, or hauling and shoveling rock and cement. This is how I funded my college expenses, working for my stepdad during the summer months.

We were a small crew of fewer than a dozen men. Another laborer, Jim, and I were the youngest in our late teens. My stepdad or Vic assigned particular jobs, such as the crew supervisor. On this day, Jim was posted to drill a hole in the concrete barrier of the bridge we were repairing. He was standing between the train track rails, operating a jackhammer. Anyone familiar with jackhammers knows they make a deafening noise and vibrate vigorously.

It was early afternoon, and we had just returned to work following our lunch break. I was working beneath the rails on the opposite side of the bridge. I had gone to the tool shack to pick up something I needed when I noted that a fast freight train was approaching, and my Jim was still standing between the tracks with goggles over his eyes and the jackhammer noisily hammering away. Jesus…what the hell is going on here? Why hadn't someone ensured that Jim left his position between the tracks? After all, our bosses were aware of the train schedules. No…this cannot be happening. Jim shouldn't be there. As it happened, he was facing the direction from which the train was speeding toward him. I was on the other side of the street that ran beneath the bridge and had no opportunity to get to Jim, but I was yelling at the top of my lungs for him to jump out of the way. But, of course, over the "clattering" of the jackhammer, my voice, no matter how loud, could not be heard by Jim.

Just moments before impact, the engineer observed Jim's precarious position between the tracks and began blowing the train's shrill warning whistle. But, of course, to no avail over the deafening noise of the jackhammer. When the speeding train was just yards away, Jim looked up and realized he was face-to-face with the end of his young life. When the train hit him, Jim's body flew through the air like a rag doll, landing in a grassy area near the bridge. Oh my God…this can't be happening. I was stunned and in utter shock at what I had just witnessed. Jim, indeed, cannot have survived the impact of that horrendous collision with tons of steel. Sadly, I was correct. I could not bring myself to approach Jim's lifeless body but trembled in disbelief at what I had just witnessed. My doubt soon transformed into anger as, after viewing Jim's lifeless body being lifted into an ambulance and driven away from the job site, less than an hour after the tragic event, Vic ordered us back on the job as if nothing had happened. What the hell? Is that all one of our crew members' lives worth it? Forget about it and get back to work because you are "still on the clock?" I also suffered, for a time, from survival guilt, knowing that for the "luck of the draw," that could very well have been me standing there between the tracks with the jackhammer rattling away the last minutes of my life. And, even to this day, the shrill whistle of a train hauntingly sends shivers up and down my spine.

In the years since this horrendous tragedy, I have read differing views about the appropriate response. Some argue that we should have shut the job down for the rest of the day in such a situation. Others propose that it is best to "get back on the horse" and go on about our lives. I cannot agree with the latter because I think life, in all forms, is precious and should never be relegated to mere insignificance or unimportance.

LESSON LEARNED

Unfortunately, the "big business" corporate attitude often values the economics of life more than life itself.

From Mechanical Engineer To TV Producer...But Three Credits Short

After graduating from high school in my rural hometown of Rich Hill, Missouri, I moved to Chicago and went to work as a laborer repairing concrete overpasses for the GM&O Railroad. I became a card-carrying Hod Carriers General Laborers Local No 242 member, making $1.17 per hour. Back in 1953, that was big money, especially for a still-green, wet-behind-the-ears farm boy from Missouri. I was on top of the world and had no plans to continue my education. My biggest ambition was to save enough money to buy one of those bright, shiny cars that the used-car salesmen "hawked" on local television every night. Even though televised only on black and white TV, they looked stunning. Especially inviting were the convertibles. Then, I returned home for a visit over the Christmas holidays and discovered my dad's disappointment in me for not planning to go to college. So, I decided to sit down and talk with myself.

I plotted my approach. I didn't want to attend college but felt guilty for disappointing my dad. So, I came up with this plan. I would go to college for one year, then tell my dad that higher education wasn't for me and drop out. I would go back to work in construction and "get my hands on" that dream car so vivid in my memory. I decided to enroll at the University of Missouri (Mizzou) mainly because I had kept my residence in the state, and tuition, unlike today, was inexpensive and affordable. But what would be my major? I had no clue. So, I took classes with no declared major for the first year. I went back to work on construction when summer came and surprisingly discovered, in short order, that "I'll be damned" college is for me....not because of what I was learning but because of the beer-drinking, carousing social life I had discovered on campus. Going back to work suddenly didn't hold the same charm it had held for me before I could live the "good life" of a college student. I could hardly wait to get back to school in the fall. But the time had come for me to declare a major if I was going to plan on acquiring a degree. But what? I didn't have the foggiest idea. But then I recalled something that helped me come to a decision. While working as a laborer – shoveling gravel, digging holes with a jackhammer, and pouring concrete in the blazing summer sun- I remembered that a man from the company's head office came to the job site every two or three weeks. He wore a white shirt and tie and did nothing but walk around inspecting our work for about 30 minutes, talk with the superintendent, and then get back in his expensive car and drive away. I only knew him by his first name, Scott. But I also had been told by others I worked with that he was a mechanical engineer and made $10,000 a year. Wow! $10,000 a year. So, my mind is made up…I will become a mechanical engineer and "roll in the dough." Yeah!

Good idea, but it wasn't long before algebra and chemistry did me in. I simply couldn't wrap my head around these subjects and, as a result, barely passed chemistry with a D- grade and flunked algebra altogether. Okay, I guess I will not become a mechanical engineer after all. So, where do I go from here? I want to continue the lifestyle of a college student. The beer still flows, and I hang out with a great group of urbanized buddies from the St. Louis area. As fate would have it, I, at the time, was dating a very savvy young lady, a former student at Vassar College and a Pi Phi by the name of Jeannette. She, quite tutorially, advised me to pursue a degree in speech and drama. Why hadn't I come to that conclusion on my own? I was a pretty accomplished amateur singer – having been a member of my high school boys' choir, played leading roles in a couple of high school plays, and walked away with top honors in state-sponsored public speaking contests during my high school years. Duh!

Long story short, I continued my education at Mizzou in the speech and drama department with a concentration of studies in radio and TV production. I thoroughly enjoyed my classes, joined the drama club, and played the supporting male role in an all-student presentation of Kiss Me Kate and lesser roles in other plays. My studies

29

prepared me for a successful career in broadcasting and advertising. But I get ahead of myself. When it came time to graduate, I had just enough credits – none to spare. But three of those credits were in mechanical drawing, a course I had taken while planning to become a mechanical engineer. My counselor called me into his office to discuss why those credits should be counted toward a degree in speech and drama.

"If you can convince me how you can apply what you learned in mechanical drawing to a career in radio and TV production, I will allow the credits to be counted towards your degree, Mr. Smith," declared my counselor. Where my answer came from still baffles me. Still, I promptly replied, with confidence, that I had learned to write legibly in block letters in the mechanical drawing course, and in my TV career, I would use this skill to hand print cue cards so they could easily be read by on-camera talent.

"Good enough for me," replied my counselor. Credits applied. Graduation assured. Thank goodness those were the days before teleprompters.

LESSON LEARNED

Surprisingly, there are occasions in life when you need not prepare. Answers come spontaneously.

IF IT ISN'T FAIR...FIND AN EQUALLY UNFAIR WAY TO GET AROUND IT

In my undergraduate years at the University of Missouri, I attended classes during the mid-1950s. Admittedly, it was an era of the "dark ages" regarding technology as we know it today. A good example is how we students registered for our classes each semester. Unlike how we currently register for classes, including doing so efficiently via the internet, over a half-century ago, things were quite different in the class registration process. Professors would set up booths in the gymnasium, similar to an indoor swap meet, and students would go from booth to booth, discuss the features and obligations of the class with the professor, and then decide whether or not to register for the class.

Entry to the gymnasium was closed to students until a designated opening time, with campus guards stationed at the doors to make sure no one was allowed in advance. Students were then admitted throughout the day according to the "first letter of their last name," starting with the letter "A" and advancing through the alphabet as the hours passed. With my last name being Smith, I wasn't allowed in the gym until later in the day, and all too often, I would find that some of the classes I wanted to take would already be filled and closed by the time I was admitted in. Those in charge of the system never found it appropriate to alternately start with "Z" instead of "A" to be equitable and fair.

So, to ensure I would have a better chance of getting into classes I either needed or preferred, I devised a method to "beat the system."

Student assistants helped with the registration process during the day, and these students were allowed in the gymnasium before the designated opening time. After observing how these students were dressed, I would mirror their attire and dress in a sports jacket and tie and join a group of "legitimate" student assistants waiting to be

31

let in before the designated opening. Fortunately, there was no ID checking process in place, and my access to entry, along with the others, was easy and without question. Once inside the gymnasium, I would "hide out" in the restroom until the registration process commenced. I then would begin my registration easily, obtaining acceptance to the courses I needed or wanted. Surprisingly, no professors questioned my early admittance even though I wasn't scheduled to be admitted until later. I used this personally designed registration procedure for several semesters in my junior and senior years at Mizzou. It worked without fail.

By the way, I found no problem rationalizing the justification for my "breaking of the rules" in this approach because, in my mind, the registration system was "rigged" and unfair to those of us whose names started with letters towards the end of the alphabet.

LESSON LEARNED

There are occasions in our lives when we find it more prudent to proceed with the intent to "ask for forgiveness" instead of "asking for permission."

Sometimes, Being A "Smart Aleck" Will Come Back And "Kick" You In The Tuchus

I attended classes as an undergraduate at the University of Missouri during the 1950s while the United States was armed in the Korean conflict (officially never declared war). It was also a time when all male residents of the U.S. were required to register for the Selective Service draft upon attaining the age of 18. For reasons I still do not understand, male college students were entitled to an II-S deferment from the draft as long as they maintained an acceptable grade level established by the federal government. Fortunately, I was able to maintain an acceptable grade level. Even so, during my junior year at Mizzou, I and several other male students were instructed to appear for physical pre-draft examinations to be conducted at a U.S. Army base in St. Louis. We boarded a bus in Columbia on a Saturday morning for what was to be a day-long procedure in St. Louis, with a returning trip to Columbia in the early evening. Without explanation, I was selected as the group leader for the journey and the day's activities. Being back in Columbia that evening was important for me because I had finally obtained a date with a girl for whom I had the "hot's" and had been pursuing an "I won't take no for an answer" attitude for several weeks.

The day turned out to be highly frustrating – strip naked and stand in line, spread your cheeks, hurry up, wait, run, stoop, cough, open wide, etc. – and all under the commanding orders of a bunch of Sergeants eager to show us "college boys" who was really in charge. Part of the examination included filling out a lengthy form to determine an individual's physical and emotional conditions. One of the questions was: "Have you ever considered suicide?" I smugly marked "yes." Shortly after turning in my form and responding to orders to return to my group, I was called to an officer's desk to answer additional questions. Standing before the officer in my birthday suit, naked as a jaybird, the officer growled, "I see you have considered suicide." I, in my best imitation of actor James Dean (my role model at the time), stood with my hands behind my back, with an attitude of aloofness, alternatively gazing at the ceiling and then at my feet, finally mumbled a perturbed "yep, sure have."

"Mr. Smith, you will stay overnight with us in the barracks and report to the psychiatrist's office in the morning for a review and evaluation." Holy shit…what have I gotten myself into now? The rest of the students boarded the bus and headed back to Columbia while I was escorted to my bunk for the night and given instructions to show up for chow. I, the appointed leader, was left behind. What about my important date back at Mizzou?

The following morning, bright and early, I reported to the psychiatrist's office, fully clothed this time and with a reflective, self-deflated attitude. I explained that while I had marked the suicide question "yes," I was just being honest in my opinion that, in all probability, most everyone has considered suicide. But would I seriously believe in "doing myself in?" Absolutely not! All in all, the interview lasted less than 5 minutes, and I was dismissed with instructions to where I could get a pass for my return trip to Columbia via a regularly scheduled Greyhound bus.

In addition to spending a crappy night in an army barracks (the closest I ever came to being in the armed services), I could never get another date with the then "girl of my dreams."

LESSON LEARNED

It is better not to let your frustration dictate your spur-of-the-moment response because the results can worsen matters without careful consideration before responding.

I KNOW YOU DIDN'T DO IT, BUT WHY DID YOU DO IT?

The year was 1958, and I was in my junior year at the University of Missouri when I found myself in a criminal lineup at the local police station.

It all happened unexpectedly when the police arrived one evening at the campus dorm where I resided and, with no explanation, told me I needed to accompany them to the police station for questioning.

Questioning for what, I repeatedly asked? My question went unanswered while my anxiety level reached uncharted heights, and my mouth became dryer than the Sahara Desert during the 15-minute ride to the police station. I also was sweating like a "hooker in church," to use a popular Southernism to explain my alarmed and stressed-out apprehension due to this perplexing nightmare being thrust upon me by the situation I found myself in.

Once we arrived at the police station, I was taken to the basement and ordered to enter a lighted chamber behind a one-way glass mirror. I found myself in a police lineup with four other young men. After standing there for what seemed like hours, but probably no more than 15-20 minutes, I was startled by a gruff male voice over the loudspeaker sound system in the chamber. Finally, I learned what circumstances led to my precarious predicament.

It turns out that I, along with four other male students, was being observed by a local high school student who had been the victim of a kidnapping and also having been thrown in a regional area lake with intent by his kidnappers to do grave harm. The high school student reported to police that his kidnappers were Mizzou students who had abducted him off the street without explanation. He also stated that he could identify the car where he had been dumped into the trunk and transported to the lake.

I also finally learned I was in the lineup because I occasionally kept and drove a car owned by a girl I dated at Stephens College. Why did I keep her car at my dorm? Because the students at Stephens, an all-girls college, could not have cars on campus. It was this car that the high school student had identified as the one in which he was transported to the lake. He especially recalled the car had New Jersey license plates.

After remaining in the lineup for several more minutes, the chamber door was opened, and we were ordered to exit, one at a time. When it came to my turn to leave, I was confronted by a rather large officer with an obnoxious attitude. His first words to me were: "Why did you do it, Smith?" I quickly replied: "I didn't do it." His immediate snap-back was: "I know you didn't do it, Smith, but why did you do it?" I, again, responded that I had not done it. He then told me to leave the station and that they would come and get me if they wanted to talk with me again.

That was the final chapter in this awkward episode of finding myself in a criminal lineup. Never again did I hear from the police regarding the allegation that I might be a kidnapper.

LESSON LEARNED

You can stand the chance of being found guilty and charged with a crime you have not committed based on faulty evidence. And it can happen to anyone.

CONQUERING THE BIG APPLE, NOT!

My first trip to New York City was in the spring of 1957, during the summer between my junior and senior years at the University of Missouri. I was twenty-two years old at the time. But let me explain how I ended up in the Big Apple.

A friend of mine, a young female Stephens College student, had a car she needed to return to her hometown, Cherry Hill, New Jersey. She did not want to make the drive herself, so she asked if I would be willing to drive the car if she paid for the gasoline. Not wanting to make the trip alone, I solicited my good friend, Dan, to accompany me. We planned to make the trip to Cherry Hill, drop the car off to my friend, and go on to New York City, where we would find work for the summer.

Due to severely limited funds, Dan and I survived on the streets in New York for a week, trying to sleep in all-night movie theaters or on the benches in Grand Central Station. Getting any decent sleep in the uncomfortable theater seats didn't prove successful, and even though we could stretch out on the long wooden benches at Grand Central Station, the cops would come by and rouse us by rapping their nightsticks on the soles of our shoes.

After eight days on the streets, we finally had to admit that our chances of finding work weren't good and that we needed to devise an alternative plan. Dan had a sister who lived in upstate New York, so we decided to hitchhike to Syracuse, where she lived, and see if we could find work there. Our last night in New York was spent attempting to sleep on benches in Washington Square Park in Greenwich Village. (These were the days before Washington Square became dangerous due to drug addicts and dealers). However, our efforts were hampered due to light misty rain, and trying to keep dry by covering up with discarded newspapers wasn't successful. A soggy newspaper is a poor excuse for a warm blanket. It was a long night, and by the time daylight came, we both were exhausted but found our way to board public transportation through the Holland Tunnel to New Jersey, where we ended up on the Interstate near Hoboken with our "thumbs up."

It wasn't very long until a young man stopped for us. Dan climbed in the backseat and immediately "sacked out," I sat in the front next to the driver. With the window down, I remember leaning my head on the door and falling asleep, but not before the wind blew my cap off (funny how we remember such trivia from the past). The young man who picked us up said he worked in the City and was going home to spend the weekend with his parents, who lived in Scranton, Pennsylvania.

After going with limited sleep for several days, Dan and I must have slumbered soundly for at least an hour or two. When I awoke, we were pulling into the driveway of a suburban home. The young man said, "This is where my parents live. You are invited to spend the night with us and then continue on your way in the morning." Wow! Can you believe it? Things like this just don't happen!

We were treated to dinner with the young man and his parents. After bathing for the first time in several days, we then enjoyed the first night of good sleep in many a night, in real beds. The following day, we were served breakfast, and then the young man drove us to the Interstate and dropped us off, where we continued on our way to Syracuse.

We made it to Syracuse without any fanfare. After a few days with Dan's sister, I was unsuccessful in finding work. I decided the best thing to do was get to Joliet, Illinois (near Chicago), where I could take up residence with my mom and stepdad for the summer and work for my stepdad in construction. So, I started solo, hitchhiking from Syracuse, New York, to Joliet, Illinois…a little over 700 miles.

I don't remember how many different rides it took me to make the trip. However, I remember three rides quite vividly, even though it is now nearly 60 years later. The first: I had made it to Pittsfield, Pennsylvania, and it was around midnight when a carload of young people stopped and picked me up. The car was so crowded that I could barely fit in. Immediately after accepting the ride and getting in the car, I suspected I had made a big mistake and that these kids had stopped for me simply to give me a hard time with harassment or, possibly worse. Thankfully, I was mistaken, and after a short ride to the outskirts of town, I was dropped off at the onramp to the Turnpike. I stood there at that onramp in a misty rain until 3 a.m. before anyone stopped to offer me a ride. Talk about being miserable. After getting in the car and telling the sole occupant, a male driver, that I was heading for Chicago, he told me I was "in luck" because he was heading for California and would be happy to drop me off at my destination. Then, about 30 minutes later, the man said he was sleepy and asked me to drive while he caught a few "winks." I agreed, so he pulled over, and I took the wheel while he climbed in the backseat. I drove for about 3 hours and, noting that the gas was getting low, pulled off the Interstate at Howard Johnson's to refuel. I roused the guy out of the backseat, and while I pumped gas, he went to the restroom. After a few minutes, he returned and said, "Hey, guy. I apologize, but I am not going to California after all. I fought with my wife last night, had a few beers, and took off. Now that I have sobered up, I am going to turn around and go back home."

So, I went back to the side of the road with my "thumb up." The time now was about 6 a.m., and I was somewhere in Ohio. It didn't take long before I got my next and final ride…this time for real, to Chicago. I remember that the car had seen better days and that the back of the front seat was propped up with a two-by-four wedged in the backseat. Again, the sole occupant was a man with the radio blasting classical music. He often took both hands off the steering wheel to conduct the orchestra for a few seconds…then back to the mundane necessity of keeping the car on course.

About a half-day later, I was dropped off in Chicago, where I caught a Greyhound bus to Joliet. I spent the summer working for my stepdad before returning to Mizzou for my final year of undergraduate study.

LESSON LEARNED

In this case, two lessons were learned. First, some people will go out of their way to do good things for strangers, and second, youth often undertake an adventure that those more mature would never entertain.

"The Afternoon Season of A Storied Life."

"Every season of your life will be an opportunity for you to learn and grow. Don't celebrate the good without celebrating the bad because they both work together to prepare you for the next season of your life."

—Theresa Lewis

Following is a collection of the short stories of the afternoon season of my life, from the start of my professional career through retirement.

WHO DO YOU THINK YOU ARE, YOUNG MAN

I graduated from the University of Missouri in 1958 with a bachelor's degree in speech and drama. It was a compelling time for me as I looked forward to starting my career in broadcasting. Fortunately, soon after graduation, I landed a job as a disc jockey at KBIA radio in Columbia, Missouri, the same community where the Mizzou campus is located. With much expectation and anxiety, I was looking forward to getting started in the industry I had chosen for my career.

After a couple of years, I responded to an ad for an announcing job at a radio station in another small Missouri market, Sedalia. I sent my application through the mail, with a tape of my announcing talent and a letter describing my experience and stating the minimum salary required to accept the position. I was confident in my abilities and knew the minimum amount of money I would need to support myself and my family, including my 4-year-old adopted daughter. I felt it only fair to establish that fact early on in the process to not waste anyone's time.

How wrong could I have been? The response letter I received from the station manager differed from what I had expected. He not only criticized me as a young man with lots to learn but chastised me for being so bold as to advise him what my salary would need to be. How dare I. That was something to be determined by him, not me, an arrogant young whipper snapper with much to learn. The letter was written sternly and condescendingly to teach me an important lesson. The tone of his letter took me aback, and I felt attacked for something I sincerely believed to be appropriate.

It made me angry, and Initially, I was prepared to throw the terrible letter in the trash and forget about the painful episode. However, as I was about to crush the letter with my hands and get rid of it forever, something compelled me to keep it instead. I then put it in the drawer of my bedside nightstand and would open it periodically,

42

read it, and use it to motivate me to prove that ignorant station manager wrong. That he would never witness how wrong he was did not deter me. It only strengthened my resolve to succeed, not to impress this A-hole station manager, but to prove that I could and would be an achiever.

From that moment on, I was determined to succeed in the industry and prove that it was right to state the required salary I had requested. I worked hard, went on to be hired by three other radio stations, and eventually landed a job in one of the major cities in America - Los Angeles, California. Later, I founded and operated a successful advertising agency for years. Upon retirement, I and my family moved to one of the most prestigious communities in America, Palm Springs. I will be the first to admit my path to success wasn't easy for me, and sometimes I felt like giving up. But every time I felt discouraged, I would stop, think back to that detested letter, and remind myself of the determination and grit it instilled in me.

LESSON LEARNED

Sometimes, something negative in life can serve as the motivator that drives a person to succeed.

KEELING VS. WINNING, AND I GET THE LAST LAUGH

In the winter of 1960, I was 25 years old and a local sales representative for the radio station KHMO in Hannibal, Missouri. I had two women's ready-to-wear retail stores on my account list, one actively running a schedule of commercials on the station and the other never using our station to promote the store.

The name of the store that was advertising was Keelings, and the name of the yet-to-advertise store was Winnings. Mr. Keeling, the owner of Keelings, was a true gentleman who, even though he had a severe back injury that caused him to permanently be bent over, with an appearance of always being in pain, nonetheless welcomed my visits with warmth and cheerfulness.

Different from Mr. Winning. No way! He was grumpy and never had a good word for anybody or anything. In my never-give-up approach to being successful in my job, I came up with the idea to produce a home-made jingle for Winnings, which I was sure would be the catalyst necessary to entice him to sign a contract and start an advertising campaign on KHMO. Being an amateur singer, I found a 60-second music bed in the station's production library. I tape-recorded my voice to the music, utilizing lyrics I had personally composed for the jingle, which was themed on spelling out the name W-I-N-N-I-N-G-S. I was so proud of myself. "This is going to do the job if anything will."

Basking in my self-aggrandizement for being such a creative genius, I was on cloud nine and fused with high, positive expectations.

After several phone calls, I secured an appointment to meet with Mr. Winning by telling him I had some exciting news to share. I distinctly remember, even though it was fifty-five years later, and it was snowing the day of my appointment. But as the saying goes, "Come rain, hail or snow…a salesman must keep his appointment." I know, but I'm applying for an artistic license here.

I bundled up in my overcoat, scarf, cap, and gloves….toting my trusty 20-lb. Wollensak reel-to-reel tape recorder…and trippingly waltzed to the Winnings store for my prize-winning performance.

After shedding my winter garments, plugging in the Wollensak, and threading the tape reel, I pushed the start button and sat back, waiting for the praise. After the jingle had played out, Mr. Winning looked me in the eye and said…"That is stupid." Talk about a dose of reality. I'm sure you could have heard the air escaping my deflated posture. I had nothing to do but gather my belongings and leave the premises with that "proverbial tail" tucked between my legs.

As I trekked back to the station, my anger began to mount, and now, I am sure, "smoke began rising out of my ears." Back at the station, I stomped into the office of station manager Jim and demanded that the Winnings store be taken off my account list. After hearing my "sorry tale of failure," Jim patted me on the back and said…"We'll talk about it later, okay?"

After a few days of "licking my wounds," I devised a face-saving idea. The number of letters in the name Keelings was the same as in the name Winnings. I re-recorded the jingle I had prepared for Winnings but instead inserted the name Keelings...K-E-E-L-I-N-G-S. I then took it to Mr. Keeling with the announcement that I had recorded a personalized jingle for all the commercials running on our station because he was such a good advertiser. And it was a bonus…no charge. Mr. Keeling liked it, thanked me, and said to start using the jingle immediately.

Weeks passed, and I avoided walking by the Winnings store, electing to cross the street whenever I came near the place. Then, one afternoon, Jim called me into his office and said he had something to tell me. He had just returned from a Chamber of Commerce luncheon, where Mr. Keeling and Mr. Winning were members. Mr.

Winning and several other members were seated when Mr. Keeling, somewhat belated, walked into the room. Upon his entrance, the other members rose to their feet and started singing the Keelings jingle, which had been running on the air for a few weeks. The incident ended with applause and a bow by Mr. Keeling. Meanwhile, Jim told me Mr. Winning seemed to shrink lower in his chair by observing the honor bestowed upon his competitor, Mr. Keeling.

Not long after, I left KHMO to work as a disc Jockey at radio station KBLU in Yuma, Arizona. I never again stepped foot in the Winnings store and lost no sleep by not doing so. However, I have a word of description for Mr. Winning...schmuck for inappropriate recognition.

LESSON LEARNED

There is justice in the world… sometimes even in small, insignificant doses.

GO WEST, YOUNG MAN!

The year was 1961. The month was July. I was 25 years old and working as a local time salesperson for radio station KHMO in Hannibal, Missouri. While my job was secure and my salary was enough to keep my family housed and fed, with a little left over for doing things we enjoyed, like going to drive-in theaters or ordering pizza for dinner once in a while, I still had the yearning to heed Horace Greeley's instruction to "Go west, young man."

For inexplicable reasons, I had fostered the desire to live in California since, as I remember, I was about the age of 8 or 9 and living on a farm in Southern Missouri. I especially remember one January first, when I was, maybe 19 or 20, working as a construction laborer in Illinois …sitting in a small apartment with my mother and stepdad while snow piled up about knee-deep outside the window and watching the Rose Parade on TV, under sunny skies, in Southern California. I think it was then that I became determined to, one day, live in the "land of my dreams," California.

But back in 1961, I wanted to continue with my story.

In 1961, the bible of information for the radio industry was a weekly periodical, *Broadcasting*. I read this magazine religiously every week and paid particular attention to the "classified ad" section at the back, which included ads looking to hire radio personnel. This specific week, a "help wanted" ad caught my eye. I am looking for a disc jockey in Yuma, Arizona. I had never been to Yuma and knew no one near the town. But the ad was intriguing because, without being a brain surgeon, I quickly concluded that Yuma, Arizona, was much closer to California than Hannibal, Missouri.

I quickly recorded a demo tape to demonstrate my announcing style and mailed it to the station KBLU, a station with a format we, at that time, called Top 40 Radio. I was ecstatic when, a few days later, I received a letter offering me the job as the mid-morning, on-air personality (9 a.m. until noon) on KBLU. The offer, however, was contingent upon my being able to be in Yuma and on the air within three weeks. It was now the first part of August.

I accepted the job, sight unseen, and resigned from my position at KHMO. My family was four then: my wife, two children, and me. Our daughter, Deborah, was 7, and our son, Michael, was 2. We hurriedly sold or gave away all our belongings that would not fit into a small U-Haul trailer. My last day at KHMO was on a Friday. That same evening, we left Hannibal with the trailer in tow and headed for my hometown, Rich Hill, Missouri, to say goodbye to my family. We stayed overnight with my parents and, early the following day, started our trek west to Yuma. Our car then was a 1957 Ford with very few comfort amenities. One important comfort feature we did without was air conditioning.

Remember, it was August, and the closer we got to Yuma, the higher the temperature rose. I remember soaking towels in water and hanging them in the windows to give us, especially our two young children, some relief from the hot, sweltering heat as we drove through Texas and New Mexico.

We pulled into Yuma on Monday afternoon, checked into the Stardust Motel, and I went on air at 9 a.m. the following morning. Coincidentally, the studios for KBLU were located in the same motel, occupying two adjoining rooms. I worked the following Saturday to make up for not being on the air on Monday. So, I took advantage of every work day between my departure from KHMO and joining KBLU.

As an aside, I took the on-air name Terry Wayne because the announcer I replaced at the station was Lee Smith, and I didn't want to be "just another Smith." I named my three-hour program "The Terry-Go-Round" and, with humility, am proud to report that I became a local radio celebrity with a loyal audience of young residents. Soon after joining KBLU, I started sponsoring local Friday night dance hops in a rented VFW hall where I would "spin the records" we played on the radio station. I don't remember, but I think I charged $1 for admission. Unfortunately, alcohol and fights became a problem, forcing me to hire an off-duty cop to keep order and peace.

Within the first week, we found a furnished home near the radio station and settled into temperatures we had not previously experienced. While our house did not have air conditioning, it was equipped with a swamp cooler. We also covered the windows with aluminum foil to help keep the house from becoming unbearably hot.

As the saying goes, sometimes it pays to be in the right place at the right time. My being in Yuma and working at KBLU definitely ended up with me being in the right place at the right time. After about five months of working at the station, the owner/manager told me he had a construction permit to put an FM radio station on the air in Redondo Beach, California. He also told me he was about to lose the license because the FCC would not give him more time extensions to get the station on the air. Furthermore, he said he could not take the time away from managing KBLU to go to California and put the FM station on the air...so he wondered if I would be willing to move to California, get the station on the air for him, and then manage the operation. It probably took 15 seconds for me to respond with a resounding "YES."

Seven months after arriving in Yuma, my family and I moved to Manhattan Beach, California, and I put KAPP-FM (93.5) on the air. At 26, this young man finally made his way to California. I have never looked back.

LESSON LEARNED

Just as ships are not built to stay at the dock but are designed to sail uncharted waters, we humans sometimes need to leave our comfort zones to realize our dreams.

ALL IT TOOK WAS A TAXI AND TWO $20 BILLS

As I mentioned in another story in 1962, I was a disc jockey at the radio station KBLU in Yuma, Arizona. I said that the station's owner in Yuma also possessed the necessary permit to put an FM station on the air in Redondo Beach, a suburb of Los Angeles and that he had asked me to move to California and put the station on the air. There was an urgency in the matter because the last off-the-air extension, allowed by the FCC after the approval date, would run out soon. If the station was not on the air by then, the license would be negated, and the money invested in legal, engineering, and other fees required to obtain the permit would be "down the drain."

This is a story about an exploratory 3-day trip to California, arranged by the station owner before my family permanently moved to California. I took the short flight from Yuma to Los Angeles one morning, and upon landing at the LA airport, getting my luggage, and stepping up to the car rental desk, I discovered that my driver's license was not in my wallet with my cash and credit cards. I had changed wallets the night before and left my driver's license on the dresser at home in Yuma.

"What the crap. How am I going to get myself out of this self-sabotaging mess?" My first reaction, of course, was to panic. However, with full knowledge that panicking was the last thing I needed to do, I located a chair and sat down to ponder the miserable situation. Amazingly, it didn't take long for me to devise a potential solution to my dilemma. I located a phone booth with the accompanying giant phone book, attached and dangling (now a thing of the past), and flipped through the yellow pages to locate where the closet DMV was. "Great." I found one less than 10 miles from the airport. I grabbed my bag, went outside, and hailed the first cab. "I'm heading for the DMV at a such-and-such address, and please hurry," I quipped to the driver. The time was around 10 a.m. I was fortunate to find no long wait to take the written exam.

50

With nervously sweating hands, I grabbed an instructional pamphlet outlining the road rules in California, quickly read through it a couple of times, and then, with my fingers crossed and praying under my breath to the Almighty above, managed to pass the written exam. I turned in my answers and was advised I would need an on-the-road driver's test. I had anticipated this and made plans to deal with it, too. Keeping my fingers still crossed, I embarked upon the next phase of my manipulating project.

After being approached by the testing instructor, who would take a ride with me and test my safe driving skills, I hung my head in despair and said: "Sir, I have a big favor to ask of you. I delivered my sob story and asked if he would allow me to take the test in his personal vehicle. As he was shaking his head in the negative, I quickly stuck my hand in my pocket, pulled out two $20 bills, and handed them to the driving instructor for his taking. That little act was a "game changer." The rest is history. He, somewhat hesitatingly and sheepishly, took the bills and allowed me to use his personal car to take the driving test. I passed the test, immediately called a cab to return me to the car rental desk at the airport, rented my car, and went as if nothing of this horrible BS had even happened. Everything was back on track, and no one need ever know how stupid I felt in putting myself through such a painful and unnecessary experience.

TWO LESSONS LEARNED

First, we need to find ways to guard against sabotaging ourselves. Second, there usually is a solution to every problem, but it often entails creative thinking and action to make it work.

It's A Matter Of Antiquated Vs. Futuristic

The year of this writing is 2023, but this story dates back to 1962. That was the year I helped put an FM radio station on the air in a Los Angeles, California suburb and became the general manager with the option to become part owner. While AM radio was top-rated in homes and automobiles then, very few homes and practically no cars were equipped with FM radios. Operating an FM station successfully at a profitable level was a challenge.

As a new radio station manager serving the suburban area, I was invited to speak at the local Rotary Club and explain how the station would benefit the local community. I commenced my presentation by stating, "I am here today to talk about AM and FM radio. But first, let me explain the difference between AM and FM radio. AM stands for Antiquated Modulation, while FM stands for Future Modulation." In reality, AM stands for amplitude modulation, and FM stands for frequency modulation. While my definitions were fictitious and meant to be humorous, as it turns out, they were somewhat prophetic, albeit way ahead of the times.

Today, in 2023, I just read an article on the internet concerning AM radio with the headline "End of a love affair: AM radio is being removed from many new cars." It appears that AM does stand for antiquated modulation, after all.

I stayed with the station as general manager for over a year. Still, I could never profit because only a few local businesses were willing to support the station with significant advertising dollars. While the shortfall could have been better, it nonetheless required some outside monetary support from the two owners (one the owner of a radio station in Yuma, Arizona, and the other an engineer at a major radio station in Los Angeles). As a result, the owners decided they wished to divest themselves of the station and offered to sell it to me for precisely the amount of money they had invested in the station, which was less than $10,000.

While the offered price was reasonable, I, at the time, had no savings and could barely provide for my family with the meager salary I received. The only possibility for me to take advantage of the offer was to find someone to join me in ownership and put up the necessary funds to purchase. One of the announcers I had hired for the station was a young man named Jimmy Coniff. Jimmy was the son of Ray Coniff, an American bandleader, arranger, composer, and trombonist who was very popular in the 1950s and 1960s. He had his own national TV show, which aired on the CBS network for nearly ten years. Ray Coniff could easily afford the $10,000 needed and might be a good source for the funds I needed to purchase the station. I asked Jimmy if he would arrange a meeting for me with his father. He did so, and I met with Ray over lunch and laid out my proposal. He indicated some interest but advised me he would need to discuss it with others in his organization, particularly his attorney.

A few days later, I received word from Ray that he was not prepared to join me in station ownership but wished me well in my pursuit. With no other viable options, I decided to submit my resignation, walk away from potential ownership of the station, and take a job as a copywriter with an advertising agency in Los Angeles.

The station is still on the air today after changing ownership several times. For a while, I kept track of what happened with the station. I stopped in the early 1970s when I noted it had been purchased by Jack Bailey, host of the top-rated daytime network TV program Queen for a Day. The purchase price? 8 million dollars. Oh well, I tried.

LESSON LEARNED

Timing is crucial to business success as it impacts market conditions, competition, economic conditions, and technological advances. If a business introduces a service or product at the wrong time when that market is not ready for it, success is complicated.

I COULD BUY A FARM FOR THAT PRICE!

When we moved to California in 1962, we settled in Manhattan Beach, a community in the South Bay area of Los Angeles County. It is a beach community located southwest of downtown Los Angeles and, at the time, was home to many flight attendants because of its proximity to LAX (Los Angeles Airport). Back then, there were few male attendants; the descriptive term was "stewardess." However, that is not the subject of this story. It is merely an aside.

Our first abode was a tiny apartment just three blocks from the ocean, and having never lived near the salt waters of the earth, we frequented the beach often. It was a new delight for me since I had lived my life until then far from the sea. Lakes and rivers were the only bodies of water I had known and experienced.

As we approached the beach for a day in the sun, I noticed a "for sale" sign planted in the sand with a phone number. Later, after returning home, I called the number. I was not in the market to purchase real estate simply because I was curious. I learned that the plot of sand in question measured 30 feet by 90 feet, and the asking price was $30,000. What! $30,000. You have to be kidding. I could repurchase an 80-acre farm in Missouri for less than $30,000. The seller must be out of his mind. Sadly, in retrospect, I was out of my mind to come to such a closed-minded conclusion.

At the time, I didn't have the funds to purchase anything resembling real estate, and I also did not have the vision to think with an eye to the future. Today, that small parcel of sand would fetch dollars in the millions.

LESSON LEARNED

We should never confine our thinking to what we may have experienced in the past, mainly when our experience has been limited to growing up in a small community where life is somewhat sheltered from ideas that we find challenging to comprehend.

IT ALL STARTED WITH $500

The year was 1963, and we were now a family of five after the addition of another son after moving to California in 1962. We were living in a small, crowded two-bedroom apartment in Manhattan Beach. I had resigned from managing the radio station in Redondo Beach and now had a decent income as a copywriter for an advertising agency in Los Angeles.

Rather than finding and moving into another larger apartment, I decided to explore the possibility of purchasing a home, even though I needed to gain experience and more knowledge of the particulars of property transfer procedures to feel comfortable enough to engage in a transaction. Acknowledging my ignorance on the subject, I decided the best way to learn as much as possible, as quickly as possible, was to go to a real estate school that prepared individuals to pass the exam and become qualified real estate agents.

After doing my due diligence, I selected a night school in Los Angeles with a tuition fee that I could afford. For eight weeks, I traveled to Los Angeles from Manhattan Beach once a week in the evening for 2 hours of learning and testing. I completed the course and received my license. More importantly, I received the acknowledgment I needed to feel comfortable negotiating my first home purchase.

My family and I enjoyed the lifestyle of Manhattan Beach, and all agreed that we wished to remain in this community. I started scanning the local newspaper daily, looking for a house for sale by the owner. Within a short time, I discovered a home for sale just a few blocks from where we lived. An added attraction was that the house was within one block of an elementary school, so our daughter and older son could walk to school and back without concern for their safety. I called the house's owner, and we met, toured the house, and discussed the price. I agreed to be in touch within the day or so.

After running the numbers, I found the asking price of $22,000 fair, but I needed help to come up with the 20% ($4,400) necessary to qualify for a mortgage loan. However, I had learned in real estate school that it was acceptable for escrow to state that a certain amount of the down payment was paid outside of escrow. The trick was to find an escrow company willing to bend the rules and look the other way to verify that an out-of-escrow payment had been made. (While this worked in 1963, there is no way it could be accomplished now). I was successful in locating an escrow company willing to play my game. So, with only a $500 in-escrow payment and a statement by escrow that the balance of $3,900 had been paid outside of escrow, everything worked, the loan was granted, escrow closed, and we were the proud owners of our home.

From that meager beginning, and while I never exited my career in broadcasting and advertising, I relied on real estate investments as a secondary form of income and wealth accumulation. Not all transactions were economic successes; I had more success than failure. While the number of transactions escaped my memory, there were many. While I will not dwell on any of my failures, I take pride in mentioning two, which were the $1,000,000 purchase of a multi-story office building on Wilshire Blvd. (The Miracle Mile) and a profit of a quarter of a million dollars on the purchase and sale of a luxury condo located on the Avenue of the Stars in Century City. My real estate portfolio was estimated to be worth over 3 million dollars.

LESSON LEARNED

With a bit of ingenuity and a willingness to bend the rules, things can be accomplished. Additionally, I learned that a big part of success in real estate investment is the ability to read the market timing - when to buy and when to sell.

I Worked For The Los Angeles Times But Never Put It On My Resume

When I accepted the offer to move from Yuma, Arizona, to California to put KAPP-FM radio station on the air, I made it a point to do my due diligence and learn as much as possible about the South Bay communities of Los Angeles County. While the station was to be located in Redondo Beach, we decided Manhattan Beach would be our residential choice.

Our first apartment was a small, one-bedroom "hole in the wall," but it was within our budget, so we managed. In a matter of months, we found a two-bedroom apartment within a short block of our first apartment. It was the most straightforward move I have made with the ability to hand-carry our belongings from one apartment to the other. No need for a truck or trailer. But I digress. This story is about my fledging career as a radio executive with significant responsibilities at 26 and the need to take on a second job.

I finally got the radio station on the air even though it was delayed for two months because of a problem getting a tower out of Oklahoma. The year was 1962, and KAPP was now up and running with a store-front studio next to Newberry's in the South Bay Shopping Center at the corner of Artesia and Hawthorne Blvd.

In addition to my position as a radio station manager, I also took a second job with the Los Angeles Times. I took the second job because my then-wife, Judy, was pregnant with our third child, and the money I made as an FM radio station manager was not enough to pay the doctor and hospital bills for the delivery. For anyone too young to remember, FM was not a viable commercial medium then. There are no FM receivers in cars and very few in homes. So, attracting advertisers was a real "uphill" battle. We had to operate the station on a "shoestring."

Later that year, on September 11, to be exact, our son Roger was born at Little Company of Mary's Hospital in Torrance, California.

That was nearly 54 years ago. It has been a joy to witness Roger grow into the man he is today. A man with compassion and love for his family and mankind, Roger is also an animal lover and currently is pet-parent to Charcoal, a handsome rescue Rottweiler, his constant companion, living in the high desert rural area just north of Los Angeles.

Oh, about that job with the Los Angeles Times. Let me tell you about it. I signed on for paper delivery with a route of subscribers in the Palos Verdes area of the South Bay. As I recall, I had about 65 subscribers on my route and drove our second car, a Ford sedan on my route. My other car at the time was a Volkswagen Karmann Ghia convertible, which was way too small for the job. I would get up at 3 a.m., drive to a central distribution location in Redondo Beach where I would gather my papers, string tie, load them in the car, and head up the hill to Palos Verdes and "run my route."

On Sundays, because the paper was much bigger, I would have to remove the back seat from the Ford to fit all the paper. Because of their size, the Sunday papers were also much more challenging to tie.

Incidentally, I learned how to "throw" a paper from the car. You must throw it in an arc to land flat on the driveway and stay put without sliding across the cement. If it slides, it will tear the paper and make it unreadable. Isn't it amazing that some trivial things we learn stay with us forever?

After finishing my route, I would return home at about 6:30 a.m. – shower and shave, dress in my suit and tie, and play radio station manager for the day. I continued this routine for about six months until we saved enough money for Roger's birth expenses.

LESSONS LEARNED

If it's important to you, you will find a way. If not, you will find an excuse.

TWENTY INCHES OF SNOW AND NO ESCAPE FROM NYC

Dumping more than 20 inches of snow in Central Park, the blizzard of January 7 and 8, 1969, marked the second biggest snowstorm in New York City history. With winds gusting to more than 50 miles an hour, the powerful nor'easter caused widespread power outages, scores of fatalities, and $1 billion in damages from Washington, D.C., to Boston.

Thousands of travelers were stranded at city airports, bus terminals, and highway rest stops as transportation ground to a halt. I have been one of those travelers. I was in the city on business and was scheduled to fly home on January 7th. However, waking to the blizzard, it soon dawned on me that the chances of departure from my hotel in mid-Manhattan were 'slim to none'. The taxis weren't even running. The city had come to a virtual standstill. However, the one bright spot in my circumstance was that I remained in my hotel with a warm, comfortable bed, TV, and shower and was not stranded in the airport like many other unfortunate travelers.

I spent the next three days in my room, dining at the hotel restaurant, and running out of several items on the menu due to a lack of deliveries. And, of course, there was the bar where many of us 'holed up in the hotel' gathered in the afternoon and attempted to make the best of the situation.

On the morning of January 11, a few taxis had come to venture out with snow chains on the tires. It was also announced on the TV news that there was a chance that Kennedy Airport would open later in the day with a few random flights allowed to depart. After weighing my odds, I tried it and packed up for a possible escape from my 'frozen confinement' and a welcome return home to sunny Southern California. I lived in Manhattan Beach at the time. After some difficulty and frustration, I finally hailed a cab and headed to the East Side Airport Terminal, where I could check in and be transported to Kennedy Airport. Upon my arrival at the terminal, I took my place in a long line of passengers waiting to speak to an American Airlines attendant. As you can understand, much grumbling and bursts of anger were voiced as the pent-up frustration many had been experiencing during the past few days boiled over uncontrollably.

I noticed that as each individual reached the attendant counter, they were turned away, raising their arms and walking away in disgust. Many loudly and profanely declared their displeasure. Finally, it came my turn to speak to the attendant to see if any flights to Los Angeles would be leaving Kennedy. As I approached the check-in counter, I looked straight into the eyes of the attendant, who I could tell was doing all she could to hold her composure in the face of such unwarranted hostility from so many angry travelers. The first words out of my mouth were spoken softly, politely, and with a deliberate tone of compassion – "I sure wouldn't want to be on your side of the counter today." She smiled and nodded her head in agreement. "Will there be any flights departing Kennedy today for Los Angeles?" I asked.

The attendant leaned closer to me over the counter and, in almost a whisper, replied, "No, but I understand flights will soon depart for Los Angeles from Newark Airport in New Jersey."

Thanking her profusely, I exited the terminal and hailed a cab to take me to the West Side Airport Terminal, connecting me to the Newark Airport. With a bit of difficulty, the cab driver made it across town in good time. I arrived at the American Airlines check-in counter and was assured that flights to Los Angeles would be cleared for departure within the next two hours. Hooray! I am on my way at last. I was handed my ticket and, within less than an hour, was seated in the lounge area at Newark Airport, anxiously awaiting my departure. As promised, about an hour later, I was comfortably seated in my designated aisle seat aboard the flight home. In about six hours, I was on the ground at LAX, looking forward to a relaxing evening far from the 'deep freeze' I had escaped on the other side of the country just a few hours earlier.

LESSON LEARNED

You will most often be more successful in obtaining desired results if you communicate with empathy and emotional intelligence than if you do so with anger and outrage.

GET YOUR HAIRCUT...OR ELSE!

I worked at David Olen Advertising in the mid-1960s and was promoted from copywriter to account executive. The client I served was P.I.P.E. (Plumbing Industry Progress & Education), a Southern California plumbing/piping industry promotion and advertising fund. My client contact was Milt Jeanney, a well-dressed and groomed older man who, as a young man, had served as a lieutenant in the U.S. Marine Corps during World War II.

One day, after I had attended a client meeting and returned to the office, David called me into his office and advised me that Milt had called him and, in no uncertain terms, demanded that either I get my hair cut or never show up at his office again. Mind you, my hair was not that long. Sure, it did touch my ears and possibly even covered a small portion of them. But not that long. Of course, this was a matter of opinion, and in Milt's statement, my hair was too long to be acceptable, especially for an ex-Marine.

David knew that if I resisted getting my hair cut, he would have to take me off the P.I.P.E. account and possibly even terminate me since there might not be another position for me in his agency. In his wisdom, however, he told me it was my decision and left it at that. In my wisdom, I knew that I couldn't afford to be let go because I had a wife and four children to support. So, without hesitation, I told David I would see my barber the next day.

Reflecting upon this incident, I am reminded that "my hair" has been an issue for most of my adult life. For example, my hair presented a problem as a student at the University of Missouri. I had to take ROTC classes because the University was a land grant college. Therefore, all male students were required to be in the ROTC. I chose to be in the Air Force. Why? Because I thought the blue uniforms looked better than the drab olive green Army uniforms. I don't recall why I didn't select the Navy.

Anyway, back to the "hair issue." As an ROTC student, I often failed inspection and was made to march several hours due to receiving demerits for not having my hair cut appropriately – letting it grow to a length that touched my ears. For each demerit received, I had to march for one hour in a circle in a designated campus area. I probably racked up about 10 to 12 hours during my stint in Mizzou's Air Force ROTC program. By the way, I also was opposed to wearing a uniform, even the Air Force uniform, so I always arranged for my ROTC class to be the first of the day, with a free hour before my next class so I could return to my dorm and change into civilian clothes for my remaining classes of the day. That way, I didn't have to parade around campus and attend other classes in uniform.

That brings me a quick update on my current "hair affair" situation. Today, at 81, I wear my hair (what is left of it) in a ponytail. I have had the ponytail for going on 25 years now. Fortunately, in today's society, there seems to be less of a stigma when men wear their hair at any length. On several occasions, I have had strangers compliment me on my long hair. While I am unaware that I wear my hair long to make any statement, I appreciate that I haven't seen a barber for nearly a quarter of a century. My wife simply gives me a "clip up" every few weeks, along with a trimming of my bushy eyebrows.

LESSON LEARNED

In life, most of us are called upon to abide by the opinion of someone else (especially in a superior position) and forced to make decisions that we feel are unfair and with which we disagree, but due to pragmatic circumstances, we comply anyway.

THE 39-YEAR-OLD "LITTLE PERSON" AND "BABY FACE"

The year was 1962, and I was a disc jockey at KBLU in Yuma, Arizona. The station's musical format was "Top Forty" and was a minor market knockoff of KFWB in Los Angeles, which at that time also was playing "Top Forty." To better understand what songs and solo artists or groups were "top of the chart" in any given week, I would monitor KFWB at night, the only time of the day I could receive the station's signal in Yuma. Our playlist at KBLU cloned that of KFWB as closely as possible. I hosted the mid-day slot at the station under the on-air name "Terry Wayne."

In keeping with my entrepreneurial spirit, I also hosted a weekly Friday night "Dance Hop" for the young citizens in this small, somewhat isolated town in the Arizona desert, which mainly consisted of Hispanic teenagers. The dances were held at the local VFW hall, which I rented for the event, and I spun the identical records over a loudspeaker system in the hall that we were also playing on the radio at the time. The price of admission was $2, and I issued a policy of no alcohol on the premises.

Even though I attempted to maintain the "no alcohol" policy and went so far as to hire an off-duty Yuma City cop to frisk young men at the door, I was, in the end, not successful. So, after too many raucous fistfights breaking out on the dance floor, I had to give up my lucrative side job and stop hosting the Friday night dances. With no liability insurance to cover my derriere, I was concerned that the fist fights could easily lead to more severe altercations, including a possible fatal stabbing.

On another occasion, I also brought Chubby Checker to Yuma for a Saturday night performance during his time in the spotlight with his hit song, "Twist." I purchased commercial airtime on KBLU with money out of my pocket to promote the event and, due to the resounding response, rented the local high school gymnasium for Chubby's concert. Admission was $3 cash at the door, and I enlisted the help of my wife, Judy, to collect at the door. We expected a good crowd, but the number that showed up was spectacular. We ended up with several grocery bags stuffed full of $1 bills at the end of the night and, cautiously and apprehensively, drove the short distance home in our Volkswagen with the back seat filled with paper bags of money. Our concern was that we might be robbed on the way home.

These were some of the most enjoyable days of my young life at 26 years old. I enjoyed the life of a small-town radio celebrity doing what gave me lots of pleasure—playing popular songs on the radio to an attentive and enthusiastic audience.

My program's playlist included songs like "It's Now or Never" by the King of Rock and Roll, Elvis Presley; "Cathy's Clown" by the Everly Brothers; "El Paso" by Marty Robbins; "My Girl" by The Temptations; "The Great Pretender" by the Platters; and "I'm Sorry" by Brenda Lee, who, by the way, had a total of 47 chart hit songs during the 1960s.

And speaking of Brenda Lee, I started an on-air rumor that the young 16-year-old accomplished vocal artist with such a mature singing voice was a 39-year-old "Little Person." For several weeks, my prankish rumor was "the talk of the town" among teenagers in Yuma.

Fast-forward ten years. I am in Las Vegas and caught Brenda Lee in concert at one of the casino venues—I don't remember which one.

During the concert, Ms. Lee came off the stage, approached where I was seated, and sang a song directly to me – "Baby Face."

"Wow!" what a coincidence.

LESSON LEARNED

Rather than being a coincidence, I have come to understand that such an unusual event is synchronicity, a thought-provoking phenomenon defined as a meaningful coincidence—an event on the outside that speaks to something on the inside—instead of just a random occurrence.

BUSINESS IS BUSINESS, AND LOVE IS LOVE

In the early 1970s, I was employed with an advertising agency in Los Angeles. I had been with the agency for eight years, starting as a copywriter and advancing to vice president. The agency was a small, one-man operation, and the owner was the president. This left me no opportunity for further advancement, so I began considering my next possible move in the industry. One opportunity was to apply for a position with a more prominent agency where I would have more significant opportunities for further advancement. However, this was my first time working for a large organization, and the idea could have been more appealing.

Coincidentally, I was presented with an alternate possibility. One of my responsibilities at the ad agency was purchasing outdoor advertising space for clients. My representative from the Foster & Kleiser outdoor company was a young man, Ric Mandelbaum.

One day, over lunch, Ric suggested that he and I join our talents and open our advertising agency. While the idea was intriguing, it also meant I would face the challenge of succeeding in such an adventure, with a definite possibility of failure. Married with a family of four children, I was really in no position to gamble. Yet, the idea was appealing, and I realized I needed to consider it. At the time, I was in my early 30s and knew that as I grew older, the idea of going into business for myself would be more difficult. Ric was in his early 20s and much more self-confident than I was. And, being the super salesman he was, Ric insisted I join him in starting our own company. The deciding factor was realizing I had $12,000 in a company profit-sharing account. By keeping our household expenses to a minimum, I calculated that without any emergencies, our family could exist for at least one year, absent any additional income, if necessary. (Can you believe that in the early 1970s, a family of six could exist on $1,000 per month?) So, with some lingering reluctance, I told Ric, "Let's give it our best."

Ric possessed excellent sales insight, and I was an adept wordsmith, so he solicited clients, and I handled the creative end of things while we outsourced the artwork. Starting with no clients, at the end of six months, we had enough business to hire a secretary, and soon after that, each of us began to take home a modest portion of the company profit. By the end of the first year, we expanded and hired our art director. And our company was able to pay each of us a reasonable salary.

As I recall, it was about two years later that Ric and I mutually agreed to part ways, split our client roster, and pursue our advertising agencies. We accomplished our dissolution without the aid of attorneys or accountants, which speaks well for Ric and me. We both succeeded in our efforts and built respectable companies. I credit much of my success to how Ric taught me to be a successful salesperson during our time together. I particularly remember an incident when we both were with a client, and I pulled a real "salesmanship blunder," which Ric pointed out to me later with no uncertain clarity. I got the point. But that is the subject of another story altogether.

But, as is often the case, we endured ups and downs during the ensuing years. We went our different ways with little contact for quite a while, and then we both found ourselves living and working in the Palm Springs, California, area. We reconnected. I am grateful that Ric reached out financially and provided my wife and me with a free weekend vacation in San Diego during one of my low periods. It was a welcome respite. Ric and I socialized and kept in contact for the next few years. Then, we both left the Palm Springs area.

Today, Ric lives with his wife in Arizona, and I live in Texas with my wife. We speak occasionally by phone. And sadly, we both are now dealing with some health issues. Ric and my wife are confronted with that terrible, life-threatening monster, the "Big C." Ric always tells me that he, being an only child, thinks of me as his big brother and how important that is to him. It makes me proud that he expresses his feelings as such, and I can honestly say that I also think of Ric not as just a cherished friend but as family. Business brought Ric Mandelbaum and me together, but "love for each other" is our common bond a half-century later.

LESSON LEARNED

Genuine, honest love and respect between two people can withstand all obstacles over the years. For that, I am so grateful.

What Goes 'Round...Comes 'Round...And Then Comes 'Round Again

In late 1962, I successfully secured a job as a copywriter at a locally owned advertising agency in Los Angeles. The agency, David Olen Advertising, was a small shop with 16 employees. The agency specialized in "plumbing industry" accounts with a roster of several small companies, and P.I.P.E. (Plumbing Industry Progress & Education) was the primary account with billings of over $600,000 annually. This was a promotional fund for the union plumbers and pipefitters in the nine counties of Southern California.

My position as a copywriter called for me to write radio and television commercials for P.I.P.E., create a monthly newsletter for the account (for which I also took on photographer duties), and write a daily (P.I.P.E. sponsored) 5-minute radio program that announced new construction projects in Southern California. I also wrote some copy for other client ads, but my main job centered on P.I.P.E.

Within the first year and a half, I was promoted to assistant account executive on the P.I.P.E. account while still handling the copywriting duties. I was also assigned account executive responsibilities for another "plumbing industry promotion" client in Houston, Texas. I made monthly trips to Houston to service the account.

A couple of years later, the agency acquired a "plumbing industry promotion" client in San Francisco. David himself serviced this account while I took on copywriting responsibilities.

After four years with the agency, I was promoted to vice president of the company when the vice president left to open his advertising agency. My responsibilities remained the same, with "vice president" on my business card instead of "account executive/copywriter."

After eight years with the agency, I left David Olen Advertising to open my shop. I could do so because David had established a profit-sharing program for employees, and I had $12,000 in the account. I just learned that the $12,000 could be paid in one lump sum or spread out over two years in monthly installments. The choice was at David's discretion. Fortunately, he gave me a check for $12,000 upon my departure. On the other hand, had he elected the two-year payout plan, my opportunity to open my agency successfully would have evaporated on the spot. In Yiddish terms, David was a mensch (a person of integrity) in his actions toward me and my plans.

Fortunately, I was successful in opening and operating my advertising agency. Within five years, I had built it into a 25-personnel company with a roster of diverse accounts totaling over 5 million dollars in annual billing.

After I departed from David Olen Advertising, David and I lost contact. Then, in 1978, I received word that David had lost his prize account, P.I.P.E., with only the San Francisco "plumbing industry promotion" account and a couple of other small accounts left, he was facing the dissolution of his firm. I picked up the phone and invited David to join me for lunch at the Friars Club (David had sponsored me for membership in the club when I was his employee). We met, and over lunch, I invited David to join my firm as Chairman of the Board, explaining that he would retain 100% of the income from his accounts and, in return, assist me in acquiring new accounts. David gladly accepted and was set up in a corner office at Wayne E. Smith & Associates, Inc.

Things went well with the arrangement David and I had made until sadly, in 1981, he was felled with a terminal illness and passed away. Upon his demise, I was left with the accounts David had brought to my shop when he joined the firm. I took over the San Francisco "plumbing industry promotion" account and soon established a strong relationship with Joe Mazzola, the business manager of the San Francisco plumbers' union and manager of the promotion fund.

Things progressed nicely over the next several years; in 1985, my firm suffered the loss of one of our major accounts, and I faced a decision. Do I attempt to keep the shop open, cut the staff, and go after new business? Or, do I close my agency, lay off the entire team, keep the San Francisco plumbing industry account, move to the Palm Springs area where we had a second home, and assume a semi-retired lifestyle? I chose the latter. And it was a good choice. In addition to the San Francisco plumbing fund I inherited from David, I soon acquired another client: a vacation resort on Clearlake in Northern California, which the San Francisco Plumbers' Union owned.

With only one employee and a low-rent small converted-house office, my income was more significant than when I maintained my 25-employee agency. And with a lot less stress and hard work. I operated very comfortably in this semi-retired posture for the next ten years until I elected to move on from semi- to full retirement. It's a beautiful life.

LESSON LEARNED

Sometimes in life, you do a favor for someone out of compassion, with no expectation of anything in return. But as a result, something worthwhile comes to you anyway. Yes, indeed, what goes 'round...comes 'round. And it can be a good thing.

AFTER A FEW MARGARITAS, WHERE DO I SIGN

This story takes place in 1969. The advertising agency where I worked had recently moved from a downtown Los Angeles location to Hollywood on Sunset Blvd. near Vine Street. We were living in Manhattan Beach, a suburb of Los Angeles, and I drove approximately 35 miles to and from work each day.

Shortly after the office move, I drove my family to Hollywood to see our new office on Sunday. Afterward, we decided to go into the Hollywood Hills to look at the worldwide recognized legendary Hollywood sign. On the way, I noticed an "open house" sign at a home with a very attractive curb appeal. While we were sure the home's asking price was out of our financial range, we decided to look at the house out of curiosity. Surprisingly, the real estate agent told us this was an estate sale costing $40,000. We thanked the real estate agent, and while not expecting to use it, I took his business card to be polite.

After getting back in the car and heading back to Manhattan Beach, we toyed with the idea of making an offer on the home. One member of our family, our eldest daughter Deborah, wasn't with us on the trip. After returning home, we continued talking about the home and told Deborah about it. In the meantime, I broke out a bottle of Tequila and mixed up some margaritas.

After about three margaritas and more discussion about the home in Hollywood, I decided to call the real estate agent to see if we could arrange another viewing that evening, including our daughter Deborah, this time. We set a time and drove back to Hollywood.

Now, I will cut to the chase! We made an offer on the home that evening with an earnest payment of only $1,000, which was about all of our available funds. We would have to come up with another $3,000 to close the deal, and we had 60 days to do it. How could we do it? I had no idea, but with the help of the margaritas, I convinced my wife to join me in signing the papers of an offer.

Now came the heavy lifting. How in hell will we come up with the $3,000 in time? This is where I had to call upon my creative juices to make it happen. Our home in Manhattan Beach wasn't even on the market then and probably had an equity of around $1,500. We immediately put it up for sale and crossed our fingers that we would sell it in time. My second approach was to ask the owner of the advertising agency where I worked to allow me not to take my two-week vacation and get paid double for the two weeks. Fortunately, he agreed. That was another $600. My last chance to obtain the necessary funds was to get a loan on our car, which was debt-free. I took the vehicle to Household Finance for appraisal and a loan. That gave us another $450. We did sell the Manhatten Beach home in time, which netted us another $1,700. Total funds now were $3,750, including the $1,000 earnest money. Still $250 short. We cut our household expenses for a few weeks to make it happen.

Hooray, we did it! Thinking back on the event now, it most certainly did take some intestinal fortitude on my part. It could have ended up being a catastrophic episode with severe family repercussions. The home at 2800 Beachwood Drive proved a good investment and provided many years of enjoyable living for everyone in our family.

LESSON LEARNED

Sometimes, people must believe in what they can accomplish, even against challenging odds. It can be a disaster, but success is achievable with some creative "out-of-the-box" planning. A few margaritas also will help!

How Did Tisha Do It? Remains A Happy Mystery

In the early 1970s, my family and I lived on Beachwood Drive in the Hollywood Hills area of Los Angeles. Beachwood Drive winds through the canyons and is the main artery to the famous Hollywood sign within walking distance of our home. A little-known fact other than the area's residents is that at the end of Beachwood Drive, there is Sunset Ranch, a stable with horses that people can rent for a ride through the hills of Hollywood and nearby Griffith Park. At the time, an especially favorite was a Friday night group ride. Our daughter, Deborah, made that Friday night ride often.

This story is about a particular Friday night ride that ended in disappointment. Just three days before this Friday night ride, we had rescued a beautiful female German Shepard named Tisha. When I say attractive, I mean beautiful both in appearance and temperament. She took Tisha with her to show off our new family member to others on the ride whom Deborah knew from previous rides. As fate would have it, Tisha separated from the group somewhere along the passage, and Deborah came home without her. While I was upset with Deborah for taking Tisha away from the house after she had been with us for only three days, I suppressed any thought of reprimanding her because she was distraught enough at losing Tisha without my adding any more burden of guilt upon her.

All of us in the family were saddened by the fact that we, in all probability, would never see Tisha again. I was mainly fraught with disappointment that bordered on despair. I went to bed feeling helpless and hopeless. After a rough night of little sleep and unsettling anguish, I arose in the morning and went to the front door to retrieve the morning newspaper. As I opened the door, there lying on the mat outside the door was no other than – guess who – Tisha. Oh my God, how did she find her way home after living with us for only three days? It was an absolute miracle – an unobtainable dream come true. I can remember the moment like it was yesterday, even though it has now been some forty-five years in the past.

Since then, I have learned that Tisha finding her way home is one of many stories where dogs and cats can miraculously find their way home, often over a distance of many miles and sometimes even for several months. How lost pets can find their owner or their home remains a mystery to scientists. However, I have learned an interesting theory: animals have a homing instinct that enables them to find their way home using something other than the usual five senses. It is viewed as a sixth sense, unlike any mortal humans can experience. The thesis is that animals can create a "map" in their mind, which consists of landmarks, scents, sounds, and familiar territory. It's believed pets are sensitive to the earth's magnetic fields, which allows them to know which direction they're going by using an inner compass. But the question remains: how do they know which way to go? No one knows, but researchers know that the homing ability is removed if magnets are attached to a dog or cat.

Regardless of how Tisha found her way back to our house, what is more important is that she did and went on to be a loving family member until she, in old age, crossed the Rainbow Bridge to Dog Heaven.

While Tisha was a gentle giant, she could also be very off-putting with her aggressive mannerisms toward strangers. This served us well in making us feel safe even though our home was adjacent to a public stairway leading from Beachwood Drive to the street above. Our backyard opened to the public stairway, and to ensure privacy, I constructed a six-foot high gate and kept it locked. Any time a person would walk past our backyard on the public stairway, Tisha when outside the house in the yard, would jump high enough to show her head above the top of the gate with a foreboding angry growl and gnashing teeth. More than once, I observed an innocent

Tisha-deemed transgressor taken aback in frightened surprise and then sprint off in pursuit of a place of safety from our "big bad dog."

LESSON LEARNED

While we consider ourselves, as human beings, to be superior to other forms of life on earth, we must, in all humility and honesty, accept the fact that other forms of life possess unexplained abilities to accomplish feats beyond our capability.

SOME BRIGHT IDEAS ARE NOT THAT BRIGHT
AFTER ALL

When my oldest son, Michael, was about 11 or 12, he was an enthusiastic Hobo Kelly fan. Hobo Kelly was the female host of an early morning kids' TV program broadcast in Los Angeles every weekday morning in the late 1960s and early 1970s. As you might surmise, the program's set was a typical hobo camp in the forest with all the trappings of such a scene, including a campfire and menagerie of colorful characters.

Wanting to do something special for Michael, I arranged to obtain guest passes for him and me to travel to the TV station to watch Hobo Kelly do her program in person. Being an advertising executive in Los Angeles at the time and placing client advertisements on the TV station, it was a simple matter for me to obtain the invitation to be Hobo Kelly's personal guest. We awoke early on the assigned day of our invitation and drove the approximate 30 miles to the studio, bright-eyed and bushy-tailed, as goes the sage description of being alert, anxious, and eager.

I was somewhat surprised at the puzzling expression on Michael's face as we walked through the stage doors at the TV studio and took our seats with a full view of the black curtains facing us. Even though I witnessed Michael's expression turn from excitement to one of what seemed to be question and concern, I did not pry into his consciousness to determine what was going on in his adolescent brain. I thought only that maybe, in the excitement of seeing in person his idolized Hobo Kelly, he was deliberately tampering with his anticipation to keep his emotions under control. I could not have been more wrong!

As we took our seats, the studio was dark, and we could see nothing. When the lights went on, we, for the first time, got the opportunity to see Hobo Kelly sitting on a tree stump, warming her hands over the fake campfire with fake flames, and with the TV cameras, I realized the scene was not going as I had expected. Suddenly and involuntarily, Michael's mouth dropped wide open, and I could sense that he was holding back tears of what I later, sadly learned, was his dire disappointment in what he beheld in front of him. Everything was fake.

I had just unintentionally destroyed the fantasy in my son's mind that Hobo Kelly was a real hobo who lived in a real hobo camp.

After the show's ending, Michael and I made the long and awkward journey home with very few words passing between us. I, in my guilt for destroying something very special to my son, and he, in his disappointment beyond despair. Silence seemed in order at the time.

Michael and I have yet to discuss the results of our fateful trip to see Hobo Kelly on the day of the disaster. But, from that day forward, Michael never again jumped off the top tier of the bunk bed he shared with his brother, Roger – eager for me to turn on the TV so he could enjoy another episode of Hobo Kelly. The magic had been shattered.

LESSON LEARNED

Sometimes, we, as parents, think we are doing something special for our children when, in fact, we are destroying the very delicate fantasies of childhood. I learned this lesson the hard way.

CLIMB ABOARD WITH YOUR CATCH-OF-THE-DAY

With all the tragic events on cruise ships today in the mid-2020s, I have no desire to sail. However, I have been on several sea cruises, with my last voyage being over 25 years ago. My sea adventures took me to many ports of call in Mexico, Alaska, the Caribbean, and through the Panama Canal from Puerto Rico to Los Angeles.

I will always remember an unusual experience on my first cruise back in the late 1960s to Mexico. And it could have been a more pleasant experience. It was a rather harrowing experience, not to be wished on your worst enemy.

My wife and I were aboard a ship that called at several ports, including Manzanillo. Our call at Manzanillo was to last from early morning until late afternoon. With lots of time on our hands and no desire to shop with our wives for worthless souvenirs, four of us table-sharing husbands decided to charter a boat and spend the day deep-sea fishing a few miles off the coast.

After negotiating the right charter, we all climbed aboard and set sail for the high seas. Of course, as appropriate for any group of macho male adults, we brought enough beer to make the trip enjoyable. We were advised that the cruise ship would depart port promptly at 3 p.m., giving us six hours to try our luck catching loads of fish. Here, I will digress for a moment and let you know that the exact number of fish we netted was…are you ready? One!

Even though we did not have a tall-tale fishing experience, we could brag about when back on board our cruise ship, the amount of beer we had brought with us served to keep us from our disappointing catch of the day. It also served to help us ignore time. That is until our captain reminded us that it was 2:30 p.m. and we were about 45 minutes from the harbor and cruise ship. Suddenly, panic began to set among us happy-go-lucky, carefree gents as we realized there was a good chance we would be promptly late for the cruise ship departure at 3 p.m.

We immediately adopted a more serious attitude toward our actions and where we were. We hastily instructed the captain to bring her about and full-throttle back to port. As time went by and we began to realize we were probably not going to get back in time to board for departure, the level of panic and anxiety began to climb to new heights. I, in particular, experienced an explosive level of panic and worry as I realized I had not brought any form of identification or money with me on the fishing trip. What would the result be if I became stranded in Mexico without identification or money? It was probably not something I would later recall with any sense of pleasure.

As I was pacing the deck with my head in my hands and talking to my idiot self, our fishing vessel rounded the breakwater, and we could see the cruise ship already underway but not yet at high sea. Our captain pulled up alongside the cruise ship and started blasting his foghorn while the four started yelling at the top of our lungs. Fortunately, it wasn't long until we were recognized, and shortly after that, a rope ladder was lowered so we could carefully climb aboard. That proved to be another not-so-pleasant experience. By the skin of our teeth, we all evaded a disastrous slip on the wiggly and swaying rope ladder and avoided flailing into the angrily swirling and frothing waters below. After we were all safely aboard, I, for one, exhaled the most essential breath of relief in my entire life.

It wasn't until sometime later, as we and our wives gathered for dinner at our table in the dining room, that we realized we had left our one lonely little catch of the day aboard the fishing boat. Oh well, what the hell? Who likes fish anyway?

LESSON LEARNED

Being stranded in a foreign country without identification or money can be challenging and potentially dangerous. In an emergency or unexpected situation, having your identification can help authorities identify and assist you.

DADDY'S LITTLE PRINCESS, NO WAY!

The event that prompted this story took place in the early 1970s. When I had my advertising agency, one of my clients was an upscale chain of home furnishings in the Los Angeles/Orange County market for which we produced television commercials. We always had to wait until the stores closed before setting up the recording equipment, getting talent in place, etc. We always did our recordings at the downtown Los Angeles store for convenience and product placement.

This evening, my creative director scripted the commercial to show a father and his young daughter, hand in hand, strolling through the store, looking at different items and commenting about their viewing. As the producer and director, I picked a well-known and popular Los Angeles disc jockey for the role of father, and I chose to have my youngest daughter, Mya, about the age of 6, as the young daughter.

At the end of the 30-second commercial, the script called for the young daughter to catch a glimpse of a white, canopy little girl's bed and very excitedly drop her father's hand, run to the bed, bounce on it, and with a big smile deliver the line: "Look, daddy, if I had this bed, I would be your little princess!"

All went well. We wrapped in time for me to get Mya back home in time for bed. The commercial was edited and aired on some local Los Angeles TV stations. Sales for the furniture company indicated a successful campaign, and client and agency satisfaction was the hoped-for result.

At this point, I should retract my statement that "all went well." Within a week or two following the TV advertising campaign, the general manager of the furniture store chain received a scathing letter of reprimand from a rather upset female resident of the area and a TV viewer. While this particular woman had drafted the letter, she had solicited and obtained the signatures of several other ladies with whom she played bridge weekly. All told, there were about 10 or 12 signatures.

"Little girls should not want to be their daddy's little princess" was how the letter began. The opening sentence was then followed up with several paragraphs explaining why this should not be the aspiration of young girls. Still instead, they should be preparing themselves for an out-of-the-home professional career, etc., etc. In short, the letter accused the furniture company of using a misogynistic approach in its advertising. It concluded with a demand that the furniture company refrain from this insensitive stance in future advertising.

The manager was not upset with me or my agency for the oversight but appropriately suggested that we be more aware of viewer sentiment in the future. As I review the incident at the time of this writing, which is now the early 2020s, I realize that the feminist movement, which commenced in the early 1960s, got underway and needed to be dealt with to avoid offending anyone. The situation has become much more acute now than some half-century ago.

LESSON LEARNED

It is essential to communicate in a manner that is not objectionable to any particular genre. At the same time, it is also a fact that, as Abraham Lincoln is credited for saying, *"You can please some people all the time, all people some of the time, but not all people at all times."* However, you must know what you say and how you say it.

SCHOOL IN THE MOUNTAINS WITH HOTDOG

After witnessing our three older children not doing well while attending classes at Hollywood High School, it seemed abundantly clear that our youngest daughter, Mya, would do no better than her older siblings and possibly even worse. While she was a quick learner and did well in elementary school, her expected experience in high school was different. She did not assert herself well and dealt with a less-than-stellar self-image.

Fortunately, my income was sufficient to enroll Mya in a private school—not just any private school, but a college preparatory boarding school, Desert Sun School, located in mountainous Southern California in a small community, Idyllwild.

Plus, there was an available bonus to attending this school. Mya had a horse, Hotdog, boarded at a Hollywood Hills ranch within walking distance from where we lived. She spent several hours each week with Hotdog, riding with others along the hill paths toward Griffith Park. The bonus? Mya would be allowed to bring Hotdog to the boarding school with her.

Mya did not like living away from home for the first month or two, even having Hotdog with her. Her phone calls home were frequent, and she constantly begged us to allow her to come back home. I remember commenting that our phone bills each month were stained with Mya's tears. Difficult as it was, we did not buckle. Within time, Mya adjusted to her new environment, made friends, enjoyed her classes, and bonded with her teachers. All in all, life in the mountains away from family was much more enjoyable and comfortable than Mya first thought it could be.

Her years at the boarding school became increasingly a home away from home, and she thrived. Upon graduation, Mya was awarded a certificate for being the student in her 1983 graduating class of 32 who demonstrated the most remarkable growth and maturity during her years at Desert Sun School. I vividly remember sitting on the lawn during the outdoor graduation ceremony and beaming with pride at the charming young lady our daughter had grown to be.

LESSON LEARNED

Sometimes, with the benefit of wisdom, parents must make decisions that their children do not share. Being forced into a new environment can initially be challenging, but it teaches us to adapt and adjust to unfamiliar circumstances. This skill of adaptability can be helpful throughout life when facing unexpected changes or challenges. The experience also can lead to a better understanding of oneself, strengths, weaknesses, and personal goals.

ROGER'S STORY OF REDEMPTION AND RESILIENCE

Growing up, my middle son, Roger, was a terrific kid. He was thoughtful, kind, and a pleasure to be with. He and I took traditional Native American names as members of the Indian Guides' local chapter: he, Little Feather, and I, Gray Wolf. He also was a Cub Scout, with his mother being the Den Mother. No parent could ask for a better-behaved or well-adjusted kid.

However, as a teenager and into his early twenties, Roger's path was marked by turbulence and concern. Known for a somewhat rebellious streak, he navigated a labyrinth of poor decisions, leaving those who cared about him deeply worried about his future. His life was a canvas of unchecked impulses and short-term gratifications, depicting a loss of vision.

Fortunately, his life path began to change when Roger went to work for Mario, owner of a family restaurant in the Palm Springs area. Food preparation became a purpose, and he soon moved on. His passion for cooking began to take center stage. What started as an interest evolved into a calling, and he found he was very good at doing something with a purpose. The kitchen became his sanctuary, where he channeled his energy and creativity, transforming raw ingredients into culinary masterpieces.

From his mid-twenties until his early forties, Roger was at home for several years in the rush of a bustling restaurant kitchen teeming with the aroma of fine foods, including numerous Italian or French dishes, among other cuisines. Life has a way of presenting crossroads at the most unexpected turns. His passion for cooking began to take center stage. What started as an interest evolved into a calling, and eventually, he found he was good at doing something with a sense of purpose. The kitchen became his sanctuary, where he channeled his energy and creativity, transforming raw ingredients into culinary masterpieces.

Roger's dedication to his craft was upended with a critical health wake-up call. In his early forties, he was diagnosed with hepatitis C. In the prime of his life, he was confronted with the fragility of his health. In an admirable display of strength, Roger quit drinking and smoking cold turkey. Embracing a regimen of healthy living, he adhered strictly to his treatment, emerging victorious over the disease that once threatened to derail his life.

His triumph over hepatitis C was not without its costs. The side effects of long-term medication have necessitated several surgeries, marking his body with scars, each a testament to his enduring resilience. Despite these challenges, Roger continued to thrive, his spirit undiminished in the face of uncertainty.

Later in life, he exemplified selflessness and devotion. When his mother grew older with myriad health issues, he moved to be with her. He assumed the role of her caregiver, a position he fulfilled until her passing. He repaid the love and patience she had shown him throughout his wayward youth. Now in his late fifties, Roger is a testament to the power of transformation and the human spirit's capacity to overcome adversity.

LESSON LEARNED

Roger's journey is more than a tale of personal redemption; it's a transformation narrative. It demonstrates how a person, once adrift, can find their true north and chart a course to a life of purpose and fulfillment. His story is a reminder that the mistakes of youth do not define one's entire life and that it is never too late to turn the page and start a new chapter.

My Horse Didn't Come In…But I Am The Biggest Winner Ever At Santa Anita

T he year was 1977, and the month was February. At the time, I owned Wayne E. Smith & Associates, Inc., an advertising agency in Beverly Hills. Not wanting to be available on this particular day for anticipated legal service in a real estate transaction that I had become embroiled in, I decided to accept an invitation to attend a "Day at the Races" at Santa Anita Race Track sponsored by a local radio station with which my agency placed advertising for our clients. Mind you, the track was not where I hung out very often, but I did know that while you were at a race track, you were basically out of touch with the outside world. So, on this particular afternoon, it seemed a race track would be the appropriate place to "get away" from anyone looking for me.

I placed my bets during the afternoon with no significant winnings worthy of mention, enjoyed the food and drink provided by the host radio station, and visited with a few friends from other agencies and media. Sometime during the event, a friend whose name I do not remember introduced me to a group from an Orange County nightclub who were also guests of the hosting radio station. I found one young lady in the group, Debi, who was very attractive. She had dark brown hair and even darker brown eyes, which I found appealing. She also had a distinctive beauty mark near her lips that added to her charm. Debi and I exchanged small talk for the afternoon races, and after I had placed my bets for the ninth race, I decided to leave before the final bell. Before leaving, however, I handed Debi my tickets and business card and asked her to send me the winnings should my picks for the race place "in the money."

With no anticipation that Debi and I would ever cross paths again, I was pleasantly surprised when, a couple of weeks later, I received a note in the mail from her advising me that none of my tickets were winners in the ninth race. However, she also included a note and her phone number and invited me to call her should I ever find myself in Orange County. Let me note here that while I was still living in the house, my first marriage was "on the rocks," and my wife and I agreed the time was approaching when I should "move out." So, while I had no particular reason to be in Orange County on business anytime soon, I called Debi, and we made a date to meet for lunch at the Rusty Pelican Restaurant in Newport Beach.

After lunch and a few drinks, we departed the restaurant, and I walked Debi to her car. On impulse, I stopped her before she got into her vehicle and embraced her in a passionate kiss. Thankfully, Debi seemed to share that brief moment of sexual stimulation with no resistance. Afterward, on my drive back to my office, I questioned why I had made no effort to request another date with Debi. So I stopped in Long Beach, exited the freeway, and made a phone call to Debi from a round Holiday Inn Hotel, which, by the way, still stands today. Every time I pass that hotel, I am reminded of that "life-changing" phone call I made that day nearly forty years ago. Debi accepted my request for another day, but I don't recall exactly when and where. However, I remember our most crucial next date – a weekend at the romantic Madonna Inn in San Luis Obispo. During that weekend, our relationship elevated to a higher level of passion and commitment.

Debi and I dated over the next few weeks, and if I recall correctly, I moved out of the house in April of 1977, purchased and took up residence in a small one-bedroom condominium in the Century Park area of west Los Angeles. A few weeks after that, Debi moved in with me, and we set up housekeeping as a couple with no specific plans for the future, with the important exception that we both found our relationship to be comfortable, meaningful, and supported with an early but genuine love for each other.

Debi and I moved from the one-bedroom condo to a two-bedroom penthouse condominium in the same complex, then on to a condo I owned in Marina del Rey.

While unsure, we moved to Marina del Rey in 1979. We married in 1980, and our son, Justin, was born in 1982 while we still lived in Marina del Rey. We moved from Marina del Rey to the Palm Springs Resort area in 1985, where we lived for some 20 years while Justin grew to adulthood. After that, we have also lived in Las Vegas, the Boston area, and now, since 2012, in Orange County.

Why do I contend that I am the biggest winner in the history of Santa Anita? You cannot measure, in monetary winnings, the enormous amount of happiness and love that has filled my life due to being in attendance at the race track on that momentous day back in 1977.

LESSON LEARNED

What are the odds that Debi and I should meet at a race track when neither of us is a race fan? Some call it coincidence; others maintain it as a matter of synchronicity (the simultaneous occurrence of events that appear significantly related but have no discernable causal connection). Be it coincidence or synchronicity, I firmly accept it was written in the stars that Debi and I should meet and fall in love on that "day at the races" some 38 years ago.

A Visual Journey Through The Lens of My Life

Jenny, my classmate from China at Northeastern University, honored me by adopting me as her American grandpa. She has returned home and is the proud mother of a son and daughter.

"Poppy" with my precious grandson, Asher. My love for this little guy is endless.

The Grand opening of Romanos with Debra, Dee, their dad Tony, and the mayor of Rancho Mirage, CA.

Luna. I rescued her from a shelter in Houston, TX, 3 years ago. She is my lovable companion

My original collage by renowned artist Phoebe Beasley. A copy is displayed at the Smithsonian Museum in Washington, D.C.

My Great-Grandmother and Grandfather Marchello. They immigrated from Castella Monte, Italy, in the late 1800s

Joe Mazzola. My very special friend with whom I traveled to Tasmania

Being inducted into Sigma Rho Epsilon Honor Society at Northeastern University

My advertising agency's logo on the building I owned on Wilshire Blvd. in Los Angeles

Brenda Lee in Las Vegas. She came off stage and serenaded me with "Baby Face."

Graduating with my master's degree in leadership from Northeastern at the age of 75 years

I'm making a deal with Monty Hall for Variety Club, Tent 29

Grand opening of Numero Uno in Tustin, CA. Dee with local dignitaries and managers

My daughter Deborah and my son Michael early in life (1961). I love and miss them

Me with Guy Snyder and Bob Williams at the grand opening of a new In-N-Out Burger in Corona del Mar, CA

Debra and I preparing to board ship for our cruise through the Panama Canal, where we met lifelong friends George and Dolores

My first yacht, the True Love. Rumored to have once been owned by Bing Crosby

Debra and I with Numero Uno executives at the opening of our restaurant in Marina del Rey, CA

*My number 67 of only 250
Series I Clenet automobiles
manufactured. "More show
than go."*

*Rich Snyder, Bob
Williams, and me at a
photo shoot for In-N-Out
Burger*

*Debra and I preparing to
christen the Debra Beth.
She became known as the
"Party Boat" in Marina
del Rey*

*My daughter Mya
and I playing a
board game in the
galley of True Love*

*At my advertising agency,
we produced TV
commercials for clients,
and this is my idea of a
clever way to announce the
birth of our son, Justin*

PRODUCTION REPORT

Event: Birth of a Son
Title: Justin Evan Smith
Studio: Cedars Sinai Hospital, Los Angeles
Production Completion Time: 7:09 A.M., June 1, 1988
Special Effects: 7 lbs. 9 oz., 20 inches

Producer: Debra
Director: Wayne

Comments: Mother and son doing fine.
        Father bragging that it's an
        Award Winning production.

*Another look at the new
name for our 55-foot
Chris Connie*

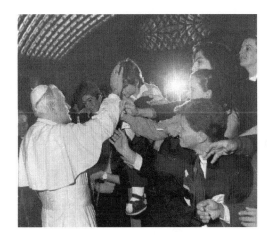

Pope John Paul II blessing our son Justin during an audience at the Vatican in Italy. Following the audience, nuns rushed to touch Justin because he had been blessed

A local newspaper article announcing the Numero Uno opening in Marina del Rey. A huge crowd attended

PAGE 28   THE ARGONAUT   FEBRUARY 12, 1981

Crowd waits in line for Numero Uno opening

Scores of people lined in front of the former O.P.'s restaurant at 425 Washington Street Tuesday, February 10th. But instead of waiting for O.P.'s to open their doors for business, the hungry and thirsty guests waited patiently for the open house celebration for the new Numero Uno.

"I sure didn't expect this size crowd," said Debra Smith, new owner of the Numero Uno Pizzeria and Italian Restaurant. "I hope our business does this well in the future."

Numero Uno Pizzeria and Italian Restaurant has other locations throughout Southern California, according to Smith.

"We had over 500 guests at the open house of Numero Uno," Smith said. "We will offer our customers different types of pizza, pasta dishes, sandwiches, salads, beer and wine."

"I guess it may be tough at first being the new kid in town," Smith admitted. "But if our business is anything like our open house, we are going to do well," Smith said. "I'm so excited."

AKA Terry Wayne on the air at KBLU in Yuma, Arizona

My business card from when I was, at age 26, the station manager of an FM radio station in Redondo Beach, CA

In 1980, under the chuppa, Debra and I vowed our love and devotion forever as husband and wife

Asher in one of Daddy's hats. He is that apple that didn't fall far from the tree

In my younger days as an advertising executive. A long way from a Missouri farm boy

Marshmellow. We found her lost and sick in Las Vegas and shared love with her for 14 years before she passed over the Rainbow Bridge in 2022

I REALLY DON'T WANT ANY MORE CHILDREN

Before my wife Debra and I married, I told her I didn't want to father any more children and that if this mattered to her, maybe matrimony would not be a good idea for us. Without hesitation, she agreed, knowing that I already had four children from my first marriage, was approaching the age of 50, and that the recent death of my oldest daughter had given me pause when it came to the potential tragedies of rearing another child.

However, we hadn't been married too long before I realized that Debra had a strong desire for the experience of motherhood. So, I had a heart-to-heart talk with myself. I noted that if I truly loved this woman, I could not deprive her of becoming a mother. And if I did, she would probably end up harboring bad feelings about me and, in all probability, would not elect to continue our marriage. The answer was not complicated. So, I had another heart-to-heart talk. This time with my wife. I told her I had changed my mind and wanted to start a family with her.

Because Debra had one ovary removed earlier, she was reluctant to think she could become pregnant. But we agreed to give it a try anyway. We read up on detecting when a woman is most receptive to impregnation. We learned that monitoring temperature and charting a woman's fertility cycle can effectively determine the exact time she will be most receptive to becoming pregnant. Before ovulation, a woman's basal body temperature is usually about 97.0 to 97.5 degrees Fahrenheit. During ovulation, a woman's body releases the hormone progesterone, which results in a slightly raised temperature a day or two after ovulation.

So, we got ourselves a chart and started the monitoring process. The month was September. The year was 1981. We planned to begin the process of fertility cycle charting as a practice trial in the first month and then get down to serious business the following month. We started monitoring Debra's temperature each morning as soon as she woke but before getting out of bed. On the morning of Saturday,

September 19, the chart indicated this was the day. Unfortunately, I had agreed to attend the grand opening of a new In-N-Out Burger restaurant in Corona (a client of my advertising firm) that morning. There wasn't enough time for us to "get down to business" before I had to leave the house. So I requested that Debra remain in bed while I was away and that I would return home as soon as possible, ready to perform my "manly duty."

As it turned out, our "practice month" became the "real month" as Debra became pregnant. Hooray—we are going to be parents in just nine more months.

At 7:09 a.m. on June 1, 1982, our son, Justin Evan, was born at Cedars Sinai Hospital in Los Angeles, California.

Little did I know at the time just what an essential life-changing event the birth of our son would be for me. It gave me a renewed life purpose. It also gave me the opportunity, with the help of my wife and the wisdom of my years, to instill in our son the critical qualities of love, compassion, happiness, ambition, and a healthy, but all too often missing, sense of self-worth.

Fast-forward to today, some 41 years later, and I conclude, with extreme pride for the man our son has become, that this was one of the most important decisions of my life: the decision to become a father again. Justin's affectionate moniker for me is "padre." With the utmost appreciation for his love, compassion, and assistance showered upon his now elderly and widowed 89-year-old padre, I am intensely grateful to have Justin as the best son I could ever wish for.

LESSON LEARNED

Sometimes, when we think we are doing something for the benefit of someone else, we end up doing something significant for ourselves.

DISCOVERING THE POWER OF FAMILY LOVE

I spent the first half of my life not understanding the power of family love. Fortunately, however, a change in my mid-forties allowed me to, very close-up, discover just how vital family love is and how it can bring unbounded joy to a person's life. There is nothing that compares.

The change in life that opened my eyes to family love and its importance occurred when I married my second wife, Debra, who came from a loving and caring family where love was abundant and expressed often and freely. Debra's mother, Marilyn, her father, Tony, and her sister, Dee, thrived on loving and being loved. That is not to say there were no typical family episodes of other expressions. However, regardless of the feelings, that foundation of pure love never wavered and always seemed to right things that may have gone wrong.

My life as a farm boy from the Midwest lacked expressed love. That does not mean there wasn't love in our family. However, it did not seem to be the center of life, as it was in Debra's family. And it was never expressed in a way that made it feel. Growing up, the center of my life seemed composed of hard work and responsibility.

Over the years of exposure to family love, as Debra and her family displayed it, I began to fully understand how powerful and vital that small four-letter word is and how we benefit immensely from loving others while also being loved by them.

Sadly, my first wife, Judy, came from an equally love-void family in the Midwest. There was barely any detection of love as a component of her and her siblings' lives. They sustained several acts of child neglect and abuse that would mean jail time for parents doing the same today. As a result of neither Judy nor I understanding or experiencing love while we were growing up, we were not adequately prepared to show family love to our children. For that, I am eternally sad even though I have since learned how to make sure love is the binding emotion of my relationships with all my children. Thankfully, they have responded to my belated ability to express my love for them and responded accordingly, ensuring that loving one another is the best way to keep our family healthy and happy.

I am so happy I learned the value of family love, even if it did not occur until later. Today, love is at the forefront of my relationships with my children, other family members, and close friends. In addition to the spoken word "love," I use hugging to express my feelings. No telephone conversation or text to my family ends without "I love you." It has become a part of my routine that I sometimes have to catch myself before ending the conversation with a stranger by stating, "I love you." To be honest, I think there have been a few times when I did not catch myself in time.

LESSON LEARNED

When parents express love, children feel secure, valued, and supported. This creates a solid emotional foundation, promoting positive self-esteem and confidence. It helps children develop a sense of belonging and a belief in their worthiness of love and affection.

SMALL, WHISPERING KISSES OF HOPE

In 1977, when the phone rang, Debra's mother, Marilyn, was visiting us in Los Angeles. It was a friend and neighbor of Marilyn's (Anne) calling to tell her that Dee, Debra's sister, while on a skiing trip to Lake Tahoe with her future husband, Dennis, had been in a severe auto accident and that Dee had suffered a severe head injury. She was in a Reno, Nevada, hospital, lying in a coma. Oh, no! Oh no…no…no!

Anne's husband, Bill, and Dennis were fellow firemen in Santa Ana. Dennis had called their house because he didn't know how to contact any of Dee's family directly.

Not only was Marilyn away from home, but Debra's and Dee's father, Tony, was away on a business trip to North Carolina. The first order of business was to contact him with the horrible news. Next, quickly pack a few necessities and grab an immediate flight to Reno for Debra, her mother, and me. Tony was hurriedly doing the same in North Carolina.

We all arrived late at night in Reno and met Dennis at the hospital, who, we discovered, had suffered broken ribs in the accident. The doctor's report on Dee's condition was inconclusive. She had suffered not only severe head injuries but also had experienced broken bones and possible internal injuries. There she lay in a coma with no ability to communicate with us, nor us with her. However, the doctor advised us to talk to Dee even though she could not respond to our voices. So, that is the routine we commenced. Each took turns to visit with Dee, talking to her without knowing if she could or could not hear us and dealing with the frightening reality that there was no way to know what the future held for Dee's recovery.

This was only a few months following my daughter Deborah's death, and I concluded that I would not be able to accept the possible demise of another family member. So, I adopted a "no way" attitude. Dee MUST recover. I would have it no other way. The others around me seemed less optimistic, and, quite frankly, I found this to arouse in me a particular impulse of anger. Come on! Dee HAD to recover. There is no other way that I will accept the outcome.

The days came and went slowly. Dee's condition seemed not to change. The doctor's prognosis remained elusive, and a cloud of "pessimism" permeated the air around me. Damn it! Don't go there! Dee WILL recover, and everything is going to be okay. Come on! I felt somewhat isolated in my insistence that Dee would heal, but even so, I would have it no other way. My mind locked on this scenario with no room for the slightest doubt.

It was the fourth or fifth day that Dee had been in the coma, and we were taking turns going into her room and talking to her with no physical evidence that she was hearing us. I took my turn, and after speaking with her for a minute or two, Dee started making kissing motions in response to my voice. Chills of excitement rushed through me like a flash of lightning. It was a fantastic break in that wall of silence we had come to reluctantly accept during the days of our one-way communication with Dee. I couldn't wait to share the good news with the others. It was the dramatic breakthrough we had all been hoping for.

Dee regained consciousness within the next couple of days and underwent further testing to determine the exact extent of her injuries. She remained in the Reno hospital for a few weeks, underwent necessary surgeries and treatment, and was then flown to a hospital near her home in Tustin, California, by air ambulance. There, she continued to receive treatment for another few weeks and was finally able to return home to continue her recovery.

Dee and Dennis live a comfortable, happy life today in Southern California's Palm Springs resort area. Dee's recovery has enabled her to enjoy the good life. I cannot, in even the slightest, take any measure of credit for Dee's recovery. This she did on her own. However, I do entertain the possibility that a stubborn, positive force working through me had something to do with that initial "connection" between us that helped her come out of the coma and assisted her on the path to recovery.

The accident happened nearly forty years ago. Still, today when I reflect on the terrifying days when Dee lay in a coma, I get goosebumps just remembering those first small, kissing motions of hope that whispered from her lips in response to my voice.

LESSON LEARNED

At times in our lives, there seem to be forces that work through us but, even so, remain beyond our comprehension.

A Meeting At Sea That Started A Life-Long Friendship

I have taken several cruises in my lifetime – some good, some not-so-good, and one memorable event that has brought me many decades of happiness. Why? My wife and I met a couple with whom we have become lifelong, close friends. I refer to the cruise we took in 1979 – a two-week cruise from the Caribbean through the Panama Canal to Los Angeles. The friends are George and Dolores Yetka, residents of Middletown, New Jersey. We became acquainted with George and Dolores because we were seated at the same table with them in the dining room, along with a Jewish couple from New York, a gay couple, if my memory serves me right, from Pennsylvania or Ohio, and a couple from my home state of Missouri. While we were friends with all at our table, something special evolved between George and Dolores and my wife and me during the two weeks we spent together. At the time, my wife and I were not yet married, and after we became close friends, Dolores revealed a few years later that she first viewed Debra and me as "this older guy and his young secretary" on a tryst-at-sea. We all laughed when Dolores finally told her initial summation of Debra's and my relationship upon meeting us.

George, Dolores, and I are all the same age, while Debra is a decade and a half younger. Even so, Debra and Dolores, in particular, have a special friendship bond that pays no attention to age but to character, love, and compassion. If there is a situation where "friends are family," this is the case with the Smiths and the Yetkas.

We are still close to the Yetkas—nearly four decades later. We have not seen them for over ten years but remain in touch across the miles. The Yetkas and we, the Smiths, have experienced happy times and sad times together. Let me share a few of them with you.

George, Dolores, and several of their children visited us sometime within the first few years following our meeting on the cruise. This is when we became acquainted and realized that this was a family we wanted to keep in our lives. So, as the years have passed, we have spent time together to celebrate special occasions.

For my wife's fortieth birthday, I surprised her by flying George and Dolores from New Jersey to California so they could surprise her with a special birthday celebration. They also traveled cross-country to help us celebrate our son Justin's Bar Mitzva.

At least two of our trips to New York City have involved spending time with George and Dolores. On one trip, we were guests in their home. We dined together in the "City" and attended the theater together. We also enjoyed an exceptional Thanksgiving dinner with them and their family one year.

The last time we were together was when George and Dolores traveled to California in their huge 40-foot-plus motorhome, and we had the opportunity to spend a few days with them.

These are some of the good times we have shared with the Yetkas. We have also been there to support one another during some not-so-good times, including the deaths of two of their children and two of my children. Whenever I think of George and Dolores Yetka, I remember the quote: *True friends make the bad times good and the good times unforgettable.*

LESSON LEARNED

There are only a few times during one's life that you meet someone who you quickly realize is exceptional and with whom you know you want to be a part of your life, always. George and Dolores are two of those special people.

A Hole In The Water Where I Didn't Pour My Money

In the mid-1970s, I owned a 55-foot Chris Craft Constellation yacht. I came to own the yacht through a real estate transaction. My first words: "What the hell am I going to do with a large yacht? The biggest water vessel I had ever piloted was a 17-foot ski boat." The first order of business was to secure a mooring for the yacht in Marina del Rey Harbor. Surprise, surprise. Moorings did not come with purchasing a boat or yacht in the harbor, even though it was docked there under previous ownership. And because of the yacht's size, I needed an end tie. These were limited and in high demand. What to do? Quick answer: $10,000 cash under the table to the Harbor Master and the deal was done.

The yacht I now owned was the "True Love;" to my knowledge, it was once owned by the famous crooner Bing Crosby. She was a wooden hull craft built in the early 1960s with teak decks. Fortunately, I could retain the services of True Love's skipper under previous ownership, Vic. He was a seasoned "man of the sea" with an honest respect for the ocean and whose only liability was a penchant for "too much sauce at times." Even so, I never felt uneasy with Vic at the helm.

At the time, I found myself owning a large yacht; I also owned an advertising agency in Beverly Hills, so I came up with the idea that we would start a program of "reverse entertainment" wherein I, along with members of my media department, would host the staff of a different radio station or TV station for a Thursday evening harbor cruise aboard the True Love. Our guests included management and sales personnel, including the sales service team, and we plied them with food and drink for what usually ended up being about a two-to-three-hour event. After a few drinks, I would then "corner" management members on the bow of the True Love, away from the others enjoying themselves on the aft deck, and suggest what a great entertainment vehicle the True Love would be for their station to use in entertaining advertising agency personnel operating in the Los Angeles market. I would then lay out a plan where I would be willing to trade the use of True Love on a shared-use basis by the station in return for air time on the radio and/or TV station. The station would use the yacht three weeks out of each month, and I would reserve the fourth week for my agency's and my use.

My plan worked like a charm. After eight weeks of our Thursday evening harbor cruises, I had KABC Radio staff aboard. I summoned the general manager, Ben Hoberman, and sales manager, George Green, to the bow, where I presented my offer. They bought it. And I was on my way to a long and mutually beneficial arrangement that lasted for some nine years.

After about three years into my deal with KABC, the twin "cats" diesel engines in the yacht began to show signs of "trouble ahead," so I traded the True Love in on a newer, 57-foot "Chris Connie." The name of the new yacht was Dingman's Folly. I decided that name just wouldn't do, so I immediately planned to rename the new craft. George suggested that I rename the yacht the KAB-Sea. I must admit that would have been a clever name. However, I named the new yacht after my wife and christened her the "Debra Beth." I remember George asking me why I would do that, and my reply was – "It will earn me browny points in the bedroom, George."

My arrangement with KABC was a trade on a "Bare Boat" charter basis where they paid for all expenses except the slip fee and the insurance, which I could only obtain from the Lords of London. In return for their use of the yacht three-quarters of the time, my agency received $60,000 worth of air time on our choice of KABC Radio, KLOS Radio, or KABC-TV on an "as cash" basis, which meant that when we placed advertising on the stations it had to be treated as a "cash buy" and could not be pre-empted. We had no problem booking the time because KABC Radio was a perfect buy for our client, PIP Printing, and KLOS Radio was ideal for our client, In-N-Out Burger.

In addition to the two yachts making money, we also had some delightful cruises with family and friends on the waters of the Pacific off the coast of Southern California, including trips to Catalina. A special occasion I remember well is my late mother's wedding to my stepfather, Walter, aboard the Debra Beth one sunny Sunday afternoon in 1981.

I sold my agency in 1985 and, no longer having any genuine interest in owning a yacht, I also sold the Debra Beth.

A well-known adage among boat owners goes like this: "What are the two happiest days in a boat owner's life? The day he buys a boat and the day he sells the boat." Another adage serves as a definition of a boat. Here it is: "What is a boat? It is a hole in the water where you pour your money." I am pleased to state that neither of these adages applies to my yacht ownership. Over the nine years of my deal with KABC, I raked in over a half million dollars in air time, which we sold clients 100 cents on the dollar. And that was back in the 1970s and 80s. I 1assume that would equate to around $1.5 to $2 million in today's economy.

By the way, I never learned to pilot either of the yachts.

LESSON LEARNED

With ingenuity, you can turn a lemon into lemonade. Even though I detest this phrase, I will use it here anyway: "You just need to think outside the box."

MAY I HAVE A GLASS OF WATER...PLEASE?

My wife's maternal grandfather, Morris, and I had mutual respect and trust for each other, which was established from our initial meeting. Morris was an immigrant from Russia to the United States in the 1920s. He and his family settled in Chicago shortly after arriving in America. He was not educated, but he was very savvy regarding common sense or possessing "street smarts," which is often the term for describing the intelligence a person attains through everyday real-life experiences. His story evidenced an excellent example of Morris' common sense. To provide for his family, Morris took a job selling door-to-door. I don't recall precisely what he was selling; it is irrelevant to the story. The area of Chicago where Morris was "plying his wares" was, in large part, a community of black Americans, or negroes, as was the descriptive term for black Americans at the time. Remember, this was in the 1920s when segregation was the "order of the day," and blacks were prohibited from drinking from the same public water fountains that whites used. Morris's story goes like this: the first thing he did after being invited into a black family's home was ask if he could have a glass of water. No way! Is a white man willing to drink from the same glass as black folks? That was unheard of in that day and age. "This guy must be okay."

Morris' request for a drink of water denotes his willingness to "breakthrough" a significant barrier of racial segregation and demonstrates his understanding of empathy. Remember, empathy is described as the ability to understand and share the feelings of another. Empathy also forges a deep and meaningful connection, thus bridging the communication between individuals.

Empathy is an important skill set for anyone engaged in the selling process. This being said, I would expect some to view Morris' deliberate request for a drink of water as self-serving and manipulative. However, I would posit that it was a win-win situation where both he and black families benefitted from the experience.

"If you want to win a man to your cause, first convince him you are his friend."

—Abraham Lincoln

Nowhere is this truer than in selling, where one person attempts to persuade another, often a stranger, to make a decision they may not have considered before the meeting.

Regarding "book smarts vs. street smarts," I like what Scott Borkun says. Borkun states: "There is no doubt in my mind "street smarts" kicks "book smarts" in the derriere. To be street smart means you have situational awareness. You can assess your environment, who is in it, and the available angles. Being on the street, in the trenches, or whatever low-to-the-ground metaphor you prefer requires you to trust your judgment about people and what matters. Regardless of where you develop it, this skill is of great value everywhere in life you may find yourself, regardless of how far from the streets you are."

To put it differently, Morris possessed excellent practical intelligence, which he learned through personal experience and mistakes.

LESSON LEARNED

You don't have to be educated to be intelligent. This is especially true regarding having common sense or being "street smart."

A Tale Of Being Left-Handed And Hot Chocolate

Indulge me in telling another cruise ship story. It was in the late 1970s that my wife, Debra, and I took our first cruise together. It was aboard a ship departing Van Couver, Canada, for a multi-month cruise through the Panama Canal, around the entire continent of South America, and returning to port-of-departure in Canada. I booked our portion of the voyage in Van Couver with our disembarkment in Acapulco, Mexico. However, we were forced to disembark in Los Angeles due to emergency business requirements. We were advised that we would be afforded the remaining portion of our booked journey anytime within the next two years. That is the very crux of this unusual and adventurous story.

Before detailing that part of my story, let me back up and provide a few other details about this particular cruise. The cruise I had booked was on a freighter, without my wife's knowledge. You should have seen the look on her face when we arrived for departure, and she realized what appeared to be anything but a vessel that promised a luxurious sea vacation. I thought she was going to break down crying hysterically. But she quickly regained her composure and, with a stiff upper lip, decided to make the most of what she was sure would be a disappointing adventure.

Once aboard and settled in our stateroom, Debra began to calm down and put on her happy face. Some freighter ships, as did ours, board a few passengers because this gives them priority over other freighters without passengers regarding docking. We discovered that we were two of only 100 passengers onboard. Plus, we were two of only a few white people because a large group of African Americans out of Oakland, California, had booked the cruise as a special annual outing for the group. Let me stop here and proclaim, "This was my second most pleasurable cruise of many, bested only by our cruise through the Panama Canal." The atmosphere was intimate, unlike that of most cruises. We interacted joyfully with our fellow Black voyagers, especially on the dance floor each evening. Some even accused us of being dance instructors. The intimacy was especially displayed in the dining room, with everyone aboard dining with the captain at his table at least once during the cruise. Our waiter, a charming young man, was incredibly attentive to our service, which made dining much more enjoyable than the simple consummation of outstanding cuisine.

Now, I will get to the crux of my story. As I mentioned, part of our booked portion of the months-long cruise had been cut short due to business demands in Los Angeles. It was over a year before we could book the remaining amount for our cruise. As we arrived for dinner the first evening, we were smilingly greeted by the young man who had served us during the original part of our cruise several months ago. He had, in the meantime, been promoted to Maitre d.

As our new server was taking our orders, an attractive young lady, the young man who had been our server before and now was the Maitre d, came over and introduced us by name to the young lady serving us. Not only did he introduce us by name, but he also prompted her that "Mister Smith, in the morning, takes his coffee here, point to the left side of the plate, because he is left-handed. And Mrs. Smith will have hot chocolate instead of coffee. What an amazingly perfect memory. I could hardly believe my ears. Talk about being impressed! This was nothing less than astonishingly unbelievable. It was, at the same time, a most delightful and memorable event for both Debra and me.

LESSON LEARNED

Attention to detail in providing exceptional service is an essential measurement of the cache of talents possessed by anyone in a role of service to others. Remembering small pieces is an oft-overlooked investment in providing the best possible experience for those served. When exhibited, however, it can be impressive.

A RENTAL CAR AND A BAG FULL OF CASH

I was driving a rental car while my car was being serviced at the Cadillac agency in Hollywood. It was a weekday, and I went locally throughout the day, met with clients, and ran some personal errands. One such chore was to stop by my bank and retrieve a $12,000 bundle of 100-dollar bills I had stashed in my safety deposit box for safekeeping. The money was in a paper bag. Upon leaving the bank and returning to my rental car, I placed the paper bag under the driver's seat and resumed my schedule of events for the day.

Around 3 p.m., after finishing business on the road, I returned to Hollywood, returned the rental car, picked up my car, and returned to my office on Wilshire Blvd., about 12 miles from the Cadillac agency in Hollywood.

After arriving back at my office, I continued with my typical workday business, checking on the progress of a few projects in the creative department, visiting with the employees in the media department, etc., and finally, after grabbing a cup of coffee, settling in my office to return a few phone calls that had come during my time away from the office.

About thirty minutes after arriving back at the office, during my third phone call, I suddenly realized I had left the paper bag with the $12,000 in the rental car in the middle of a conversation. I slammed the phone down right in the middle of the conversation and involuntarily yielded to a staggering state of panic. I broke out in a cold sweat and felt like I was about to faint. This feeling of losing control ambushed me, and for a moment, I also became disoriented and confused, not knowing what to do next. However, fortunately, I quickly regained my senses and pulled myself together. How could I have made such a ridiculous and potentially costly error? How could I have done such an idiotic thing? I frantically located the phone number and immediately called the car rental agency. After identifying myself, I, in a fierce and trembling voice, insisted to the person who answered the phone, "Under no circumstance, do not rent that car I returned about an hour ago. I forgot something in it, and I am on my way to pick it up now."

I darted out of the office without explanation, sprinted to my car, and headed for the rental agency. I sped through the heavy afternoon traffic as if being chased by the police. I ran stop lights, blared my horn at pedestrians, and made the trip in about one-third the time it would have taken had I not broken all the safe driving rules.

Once I reached the rental agency, I dashed into the office and announced who I was and why I was there. One of the two attendants behind the counter reached down and handed me my paper bag full of President Benjamin Franklin. With my hands still shaking from the emotional state of near-hysteria I was just now coming out of, I opened the paper bag and concluded nothing was missing. I pulled two $100 bills out of the bag and handed one to each man. I thanked them and made a more sanity return to my office. This time, I found no need to drive like a maniac. Thank goodness my mission had been achieved, and a calming and welcomed sense of relief emerged.

Things could have turned out much differently. The men at the rental agency could easily have said they had already rented the car or, upon inspecting it, found nothing. I thank my lucky stars that the men at the rental car agency were honest.

LESSON LEARNED

We must be aware that we subconsciously can self-sabotage ourselves, engaging in destructive behavior directed at ourselves.

OOPS!

As I write this (March 2016), Jerry Maren is 96. Who is Jerry Maren? You may ask. Remember the munchkin who hands the big lollipop to Judy Garland in *The Wizard of Oz*? That was Jerry Maren. Why do I write about Jerry? You may ask. Because he is one of the most significant little people I have ever met. His role as a munchkin in *The Wizard of Oz* was the first of many movies and TV roles for Jerry. He worked with the Marx Brothers in the film *At The Circus*; was, along with fellow Munchkin Billy Curtis, in the movie *Little Cigars* (a gang of midgets on a crime spree); was the dapper little man on the *Gong Show*, and played an ape-child in *Battle of the Planet of the Apes*. Jerry was also the "pitchman" for several products in television commercials, including Little Oscar for the Oscar Mayer Company and Buster Brown for the Buster Brown Shoe Company. In commercials for McDonald's, Jerry portrayed Mayor McCheese and the Hamburgler.

Jerry was what, in earlier times, we called a midget. He is only four feet, three inches in height. Today, the accepted terminology for people of Jerry's stature is "Little People," a term that Jerry and his friend Billy Barty introduced as the organizers of "Little People of America." Unlike dwarfs, little people's bodies and bone structure are proportioned ordinarily, as with persons of regular size and height.

I first met Jerry in the 1970s when I engaged him to play the "Woody The Sandman" role in a television commercial for a client of my ad agency, W. Simmons Mattress Company. Not to be confused with THE Simmons Mattress Company, W. Simmons mattress company was a regional chain of mattress stores in Southern California, founded by "Woody" Simmons and operated by his son, Wayne Simmons.

I created the following scenario for the commercial featuring Jerry, which we shot at the KTLA-TV studios on Sunset Blvd. in Hollywood.

We lined up on stage, side by side, with a king-size mattress, a queen-size mattress, a full-size mattress, a twin-size mattress, and a baby crib.

Jerry is dressed in a nightcap and gown with "Woody" stitched on the shift across his chest. The commercial opens with Jerry bouncing on the king-size mattress. He announces: "Hi…I am Woody-the Sandman for W. Simmons Mattress, where you can now buy this king-size mattress for only x-$." Jerry then jumps to the queen-size mattress and continues… "Or you can buy this one for only x-$." The sequence continues with Jerry jumping from the queen-size mattress to the full-size and twin-size mattress with the same message. To bring the commercial to a close, it is scripted for Jerry to jump from the twin-size mattress to the baby crib, peek his head over the rail, announce, "Sorry, this one is not for sale, it is mine" then lay his head down and fall asleep.

Things went differently than planned. Everything was on cue until Jerry jumped from the twin-size mattress to the baby crib. When he landed in the crib, the bottom fell out with a crash. Immediately, Jerry, being the professional he is, stuck his head over the rail and squealed, "Oops!" The entire crew, including me, broke out in a loud barrage of laughter. We edited and aired the commercial as it had spontaneously happened, including Jerry's "Oops" finale. It was one of the most successful TV ads we produced for W. Simmons, generating enormous sales.

I noticed the commercial on a "TV Bloopers" program a few years later.

Jerry Maren and I became friendly following the W. Simmons Mattress TV commercial episode. Not close, intimate friends…but an acquaintance friendship of mutual respect. He is one of the kindest and most gentlemanly men I have had the pleasure of knowing. I remember being invited to his home and how interesting it was to see how the furnishings and appliances were sized for Jerry and his wife, Elizabeth, 's convenience.

Last month, I read, with sadness, on the internet that Jerry had passed away. Happily, however, it was announced the following day that this was in error. Not a hoax but simply a mistake. On Instagram, Jerry said he was "alive and well, thank you."

Jerry has a handprint, a footprint at Grauman's Chinese Theater in Hollywood, and his star on the Hollywood Walk of Fame. As I said, Jerry Maren is the biggest little person you could have the pleasure of knowing.

LESSON LEARNED

A person is a person, no matter how small. These are not my words but those of Dr. Seuss. I suspect Dr. Seuss was referring to the fact that a child, even though small, still deserves the respect of being a person. I would apply his proclamation to children and little people of all ages.

VIVA IL PAPA AND A RUSHING STAMPEDE OF NUNS

My heritage on my mother's side of the family is Italian. Her maiden name was Markello (an Americanized spelling of Marchello). Without proof, I think this incorrect spelling stems from the pronunciation of "ch" as a "k" in the Italian language. I can imagine when my great-grandmother and great-grandfather Marchello arrived at Ellis Island and were asked their surname, their verbalized answer was written down with a "k" and not a "ch." That is my speculation, but the proof is neither confirmed nor essential.

What is important is that, after yearning to visit the homeland of my maternal side of the family for as long as I can remember, the opportunity finally came in 1987. Along with my wife, Debra, and our 5-year-old son, Justin, I planned a 30-day driving tour of Italy – starting in Milan and ending in Rome – with visits to Castellamonte, the hometown of my ancestors (a small community about 22 kilometers north of Turin and located at the foot of a hill surmounted by a fourteenth-century castle, hence the name, meaning castle at the mount), Florence, Aosta Valley, Portofino, Venice, and Sorrento. With my limited ability to speak (and understand) Italian, I navigated our itinerary with minimum difficulty. And it was a most memorable and exciting adventure.

Just three days before our departure, Justin fell from his swing set in our backyard and broke a small bone in his foot. Ouch! We may have to cancel our trip. Hold on. There is good news! The doctor was able to fit him with a walking cast and assured us there would be no problem. So, onward with our plans.

I have lasting memories of all the places we visited during our visit to Italy. However, the highlight of our trip happened during our visit to Vatican City. We marveled at the Sistine Chapel and were mesmerized by the overwhelming, expansive interior and statues adorning St. Peter's Basilica. Upon stepping inside, we noted Justin observing several nuns crossing themselves as they stood before Michelangelo's Pieta, the figure of Mary and Jesus. After the nuns left, Justin stepped before the statue and emulated the nuns by crossing himself. He then noticed we were watching him, so he ran over to us and advised his mother, "I know, Mom, I'm Jewish, but nothing got through because I'm wearing my jean jacket." Out of the words of babes come unique treasures. This was one to remember.

But the exceptional occasion at the Vatican was an audience with Pope John Paul II. Debra successfully obtained tickets for the audience through the efforts of Joseph, a young priest and personal friend. When I reported we had an audience with the Pope, we three sat down for a private one-on-one conversation with il Papa. Not exactly. Along with a few hundred (maybe a thousand) others, we gathered in the Basilica auditorium and sat humbling before the Pope as he offered words of wisdom in several languages. Following his address, the Pope walked down the aisle between the rows of pews and would stop to bless select persons and objects within his reach personally.

We were seated approximately eight seats from the aisle where the Pope was traversing, and our best hope was that we would catch a brief glimpse of him as he passed our aisle. But just as the Pope approached our aisle, the young man next to us picked Justin up and handed him to the person next to him. Justin's passing-on continued from one to another until he was picked up and placed on the shoulders of the young man seated right next to the aisle and within reach of il Papa. What happened next was unbelievable. Pope John Paul II reached out and touched Justin on the forehead while offering a personal blessing. Afterward, Justin was passed back to us, and all three were in a daze. Wow! What had just happened was unimaginable but, at the same time, so spiritually fascinating. After the audience with the Pope was concluded and we departed the auditorium, several nuns rushed to Justin in near stampede mode, reaching out to touch him. Because Justin had been touched and blessed by Il Papa, the nuns expected that they would also receive the Pope's blessings by touching Justin.

But the story does not end there. The next day, we were taking a tour of the Vatican Gardens when an American tourist couple came up to us and excitedly informed us they had seen a picture of the Pope blessing our son in a display of pictures posted for purchase. We obtained from them the address where the photos were posted, located those of the Pope and Justin, and placed our order. Weeks later, after returning home, the picture arrived and has hung in a prominent place of pride in our home ever since. The Pope chose him as a blessing because of Justin's walking cast. You might say, "It was a case of a silver lining behind the cloud." In any event, it was, and is, an exceptional experience to live and relive in vivid memory as the years pass.

LESSON LEARNED

Those persons who willingly and voluntarily passed Justin to the center aisle where the Pope could reach and bless him proved that there are people in this world, even though they may be strangers, who will take it upon themselves to act with compassion and demonstrate a genuine attitude of love and selflessness.

MY "HEY, LOOK AT ME" WHEELS!

I first saw the Clénet automobile in 1975 while attending the Los Angeles Car Show with my son, Michael. I maintain it is never a good idea to love anything that cannot love you back. However, I must admit that I "fell head over heels" with unfettered and acute "attraction" for this beautiful work of art on wheels. It was luxuriously appointed, including a crystal Waterford ashtray. Magnificent! Gorgeous! Stunning! I could go on and on with an infinite string of praiseworthy adjectives to describe this alluring automobile. But I think you get the idea. I did like the looks of what I was admiring. Indeed, I did. But wishful-window shopping was all I could afford at the time. Maybe one day?

About four years later, that "one day" arrived, and I became the proud owner of number 67 of the Series One Clénet. Oh, happy day! Only 250 of these beauties were built, and I, as an owner, was in good company. Other Clénet owners included such well-known celebrities as Farrah Fawcett, Rod Stewart, Ken Norton, Sylvester Stallone, and King Hussein of Jordon. Now, not bad company, if I do say so myself.

For those who may not be familiar with Clénet, let me introduce you to a bit of history. Unfortunately, its history has a not-so-good ending. Clénet Coachworks, Inc. was formed by Alain Clénet and investors in 1975. Originally started in a garage, the company was moved into an airplane hangar where an assembly line style of production was begun, later to be reborn in a "high tech" facility in Goleta, California, where production of Series II continued until the company ran into financial difficulties in 1980, ceased production, and Alain Clénet filed for bankruptcy. The remaining bodies, tooling, and equipment went up for auction. Soon after the bankruptcy, Alfred J. DiMora, owner of Classic Clenet Club and one of the first employees of Clenet, purchased all of the assets of Clénet Coachworks, Inc. DiMora has not continued production.

Clénet's first car was, logically enough, called the Series I. It was a roadster designed in a 1930s style. This was then replaced by the heavier-looking Series II in 1979. A total of 250 factory-authorized Series I, 187 Series II, 65 Series III, and 15 Series IV cars were produced by Clenet Coachworks, Inc. Clénets sold for around US $75,000 in the 1970s. I still think the Series 1 Clénet is one of the best-looking cars ever built, but I must admit that its beauty is better viewed from afar. While I enjoyed owning and driving my Clénet, I also found downsides. First of all, it was not a comfortable ride. The car's design meant you sat directly atop the rear axle, and, as a result, you felt every bump in the road. Parking in public places also created a problem. I was never comfortable parking near other cars, so I would pick a spot far away to avoid scratches or damage. I also would avoid valet parking because I didn't want anyone else behind the wheel; I remember one time when we were driving the Clénet from our home in Marina del Rey to Palm Springs, there were warnings of a possible sand storm on Highway 10 so I took a long detour through the mountainous area of Idyllwild so to avoid any potential damage to the car. It always seemed necessary to "pamper" the vehicle and treat it with special "kid glove" care. After a while, it became a tedious chore.

About five years later, I concluded that I had been there and done that…so number 67 went up for sale. The last time I checked, I believe in 2006 or 007, my Clénet was owned by a resident of Las Vegas. We lived in Las Vegas then, so I contacted the owner, who invited me to see her. But, after some deliberation with myself, I elected to pass for fear I might "fall head over heels" again by simply "sneaking a peek" at the beauty.

LESSON LEARNED

Sometimes in life, we may have a longing for something, but after we acquire it, it is not everything we had hoped for.

It's The Will, Not The Skill

Have you ever been in a situation where someone walks into the room and, immediately, you realize you are in the presence of an individual with an extraordinary, captivating personality? I think just such a person is Dr. Jim Tunney…, an educator, former NFL referee, and motivational speaker. Some term this personality quality as charisma, a word of Greek origin meaning "gift of grace" (synonyms: charm, presence, the force of personality, attractiveness, magnetism, appeal, allure). Jim exudes all of these qualities, so I conclude that it is appropriate to identify him as being charismatic. Most importantly, however, Jim relies on his charisma to make an impressive, positive impact on those he contacts.

I first met Jim Tunney in the early 1970s when he was principal at Hollywood High School, where my eldest daughter, Deborah, was a student and I was a community advisory committee member.

Jim Tunney's career is expansive, exemplary, and thriving. It includes multiple years in education, national professional sports, author, community service, and motivational speaking. He is the past president of the National Speakers Bureau and has been distinguished as the "Dean of NFL Referees" and the only NFL referee to officiate back-to-back Super Bowl games.

Visit the Premier Speakers Bureau website to learn about and review a few of Dr. Tunney's accomplishments.

"A former high school coach, teacher, principal, and district superintendent, he had a 40-year career officiating football and basketball. Thirty-one of those years, he was an NFL Referee working a record twenty-nine post-season games, including three Super Bowls, ten NFC/AFC Championship games, six Pro Bowls, and twenty-five Monday Night Games. He officiated some of the most memorable games in NFL

history, including "The Ice Bowl," "The Kick," "The 100th Bears-Packers Game," "The Snowball Game," the "Final Fumble," "The Fog Bowl," and "The Catch."

I again had the opportunity to be in the presence of Jim Tunney in the late 1970s-early 1980s when I arranged to have him speak to the employees of three of my ad agency clients. On one occasion, after arranging for Jim to talk to a client's staff at a Northern California Resort, I picked him up at the San Francisco airport and drove him to the resort and back, about two hours each way. During our one-on-one time together, I learned much about Jim's passion for motivating people to be their best. I can honestly report that those four-plus hours with Jim Tunney are the most inspiring I have had the fortune to experience

As a Professional Speaker, Jim is the Past President of the National Speakers Association and a Charter Member of its most prestigious group – The CPAE Speakers Hall of Fame. He also holds every professional designation of the NSA, including the Oscar of Professional Speaking – The Cavett.

As an author, Jim has written and/or co-authored nine books: Impartial Judgment, Chicken Soup for the Sports Fan's Soul, Speaking Secrets of the Masters, You Can Do It!, Super Bowl Sunday, Insights into Excellence, Lessons in Leadership, Build a Better You and now, It's the Will, Not the Skill.

Dr. Tunney also founded the Jim Tunney Youth Foundation, which supports local community programs that develop youth leadership, work skills, wellness, and self-esteem.

My favorite book authored by Dr. Tunney is *It's the Will, Not the Skill*, which emphasizes the importance of willpower. In the book, which details the true-life success story of NFL Head Coach Herm Edwards, Dr. Tunney argues that the will is as necessary and sometimes more than one's skill. He further asserts that a person can and will succeed by preparation, persistence, and an ever-present positive approach to life. The book is an ideal text for parents, teachers, coaches, and managers who seek to improve the self-confidence and performance of others. I treasure my copy of the book, which, by the way, is autographed by Dr. Jim Tunney.

Now in his mid-80s, Dr. Tunney lives in Pebble Beach, California, and remains active in speaking, writing, and community involvement. He also maintains a popular blog, *The Tunney Side of Sports*. One recent post on his blog is a tribute to "Omaha" – an observance of the recent retirement of Peyton Manning, where Dr. Tunney maintains that Peyton is "refiring," not "retiring."

If you were to ask me…who would I choose to be if I could not be myself?...my unhesitating answer would be "Dr. Jim Tunney."

LESSON LEARNED

Certain people you come into contact with have a lasting and positive influence on your life. These people can also become your mentor, albeit without knowing it. Jim Tunney, most certainly, has filled that role in my life.

In-N-Out...That's What A Hamburger Is All About

In the mid-1970s, my advertising agency acquired a new client. It was a small chain of hamburger fast food restaurants with only 17 outlets, all in surrounding communities of Los Angeles – the San Fernando Valley to the north, the San Gabriel Valley to the east, and Orange County to the south, with no outlets in Los Angeles proper. Why? Because In-N-Out built restaurants only on land they could purchase, the owners felt that the cost of real estate in Los Angeles was prohibitive.

In-N-Out was founded in 1948 in Baldwin Park, California (in the San Gabriel Valley) by Harry and Esther Snyder. They and their two sons, Guy and Rich, operated the small chain of eateries when we acquired the account. Sadly, within the first year of our acquiring the account, Harry Snyder was felled by cancer, leaving the operation of In-N-Out to his sons. Both Guy and Rich were in their mid-20s, with Rich, the youngest of the two, taking the helm as president of the company at 24.

While it is not my nature to be negative, I admit that at the time, I predicted that the company under the leadership of such a young man was destined for failure. I was inclined to write off the new client as a short-lived relationship but found no reason to resign without at least an opportunity to be found in error with my assumption of the firm's failure.

How "wronger" could I be? Today's little chain of 17 hamburger stands is an icon of success with 304 locations in six western states. We were the first advertising agency for In-N-Out and served as the company's advertising/marketing counsel for about ten years until I closed my agency in 1985. At that time, the chain had grown, under the guidance of Rich, to about 40 or 50 locations, all in Southern California.

Sadly, the success and growth of In-N-Out is a bitter/sweet story. Rich Snyder successfully mastered the growth of the company with expansion to 93 locations

134

when, in 1993, at the age of 41, he, along with childhood friend and Executive Vice President of the company, Philip West, was killed in a plane crash that took place as the private, chartered aircraft was on the approach for landing at John Wayne Airport in Orange County.

Rich and Philip were on a business trip and en route to John Wayne Airport, following a one-day trip, which began in Long Beach in the morning and was scheduled to end at John Wayne Airport that evening, including a stop in Fresno for the opening of a new restaurant and scouting of other potential locations in Southern California. The plane stopped in Fresno, Bakersfield, and La Verne before heading back to Orange County, where the company had recently moved its corporate headquarters to Irvine, and Rich had purchased a home in Newport Beach.

Rich's mother, Esther, also had been aboard the private jet but disembarked in La Verne about 20 miles east of Los Angeles just minutes before.

Following Rich's untimely death, the operational responsibility fell to his brother, Guy, who continued to expand the company and nurture its success. At age 49 in the year 2000, Guy died of an accidental overdose of a prescription painkiller. The number of In-N-Outs at this time was 140. Upon Guy's death, the company's management responsibilities reverted to Esther, who was 80 years of age at the time. The company continued to grow under Ether's guidance until she died in 2006 at 86. Upon Esther's death, company ownership was transferred to the only family heir, Guy's daughter Lynsi. At the time, Lynsi was 24 years old.

Today, at 33, Lynsi oversees an empire of over 300 restaurants in six states, staffed by some 17,000 employees. She has weathered personal tragedies and legal strife to helm the iconic company her grandparents founded. She has taken on the responsibility of guiding a company that has survived and thrived for more than six decades despite an assortment of competitors, ranging from multinational giant McDonald's to scores of upstarts trying to imitate the In-N-Out simplistic but high-quality version of fast food. If flipping burgers can be likened to art, Snyder's task can be compared to an expert assigned to restore a Rembrandt. She has aptly preserved and nurtured the In-N-Out brand in a 21st-century marketplace far removed and vastly different from its origins—and instinctively, she is doing it without changing an operation built on familiarity.

When Harry and Esther Snyder opened that first hamburger stand after World War II, their business plan was to sell a few simple, inexpensive menu items made from the best, freshest ingredients they could obtain and to prepare them meticulously by hand so that they tasted as good as possible. Six decades later, the formula remains the same under Lynsi's tutelage. She adheres, with determination, to the old adage… "If it ain't broke, don't fix it."

Oh yeah, back to my prediction that In-N-Out was probably doomed to failure following the death of founder Harry. Today, according to Bloomberg's ranking, the chain is valued at about $1.1 billion, and Lynsi is purported to be the youngest American female billionaire. So much for my ability to call the future.

LESSON LEARNED

Don't be quick to conclude about the success or failure of someone or something when you are basing your prediction not on facts but on assumptions. Secondly, accept that wisdom and expertise are not the domain of only the older.

YOU MAY BE THE OWNER, BUT YOU ARE NOT ALWAYS IN CHARGE

In the late 1970s, as the sole owner and proprietor of an advertising agency in Los Angeles, the sole owner and proprietor of another agency and I attempted to merge our two agencies.

The merger made economic sense because my other agency and I were specialists in the same advertising niche – retail advertising in broadcasting. The owner of the other agency was some 15 years my senior, and he desired to retire and sell out to me within five years of the merger. I aimed to build an agency with more accounts and significant revenue.

The mix of personnel talent and skills of our two agencies meshed quite effectively with no duplication or need to terminate anyone. Plus, there was only one instance of account conflict. We both had a mattress company on our roster of clients. Since the mattress account of the other agency was more prominent, with a larger advertising budget, I elected to resign from the mattress account in our shop.

As owners of the two agencies, we both understood the practicality of the merger and felt strongly that it held the promise to deliver the objectives of both the other owner and me. However, the union failed because neither I nor the other agency owner could motivate our respective employees to work together. Even though, before the merger, we brought our two staff together a couple of times as a "get to know each other" opportunity, we had not taken the time to honestly analyze our team concerning their questions, fears, and concerns. We had not done the due diligence necessary to measure the individual attitudes and willingness to work together successfully.

The "us and them" attitude became an unbearable burden on the culture of the merged agencies, so we de-merged after one year. Fortunately, we had been wise enough to keep our separate corporations intact when we formed the newly merged corporation. So, we simply put the process in reverse, separated all accounts back into each agency that brought them into the merged agency, and went our separate ways. While we owners felt the merger was an opportunity for the whole to become more significant than the sum of the parts and where we understood that preconceived notions of what we felt was achievable might be challenged, in the end, it became evident that our objective was not feasible, so we "threw in the towel." We both were operating on the concept that relationships between our staff would be built and deepened as our people came together and experienced desirable togetherness. We both had reputations for leading our people with the understanding that they respond well to being recognized for what they do and who they are.

While we owners felt the merger was an opportunity for the whole to become more significant than the sum of the parts and where we understood that preconceived notions of what we felt was achievable might be challenged, in the end, it became evident that our objective was not viable, so we, as the saying goes "threw in the towel." It was an expensive and stressful attempt, but failed miserably.

LESSON LEARNED

While you may own a business, you are not necessarily in control of everything. So, keep that in mind when attempting any significant change that involves people.

THE $300,000 LOGO MIRROR

In the 1970s and 80s, one of the clients on the roster of my advertising agency was a regional chain of pizzerias, Deep Dish Numero Uno. The chain of about 25 franchisee locations throughout Southern California was popular and successful.

After we had serviced the client with a radio and television advertising campaign for about two years, I decided to investigate becoming a franchisee. My reason for the consideration was to provide a business that could be operated by family members - my wife, her mother and father, and her sister. Instead of signing a franchise contract for one location, I went all-in and plunked down $100,000 to open and operate six sites. I never considered being involved in operations but took the lead in obtaining sites, equipping the restaurants, and marketing them. Management of the restaurants would be the responsibility of my family members.

At the time, my wife and I lived in the Los Angeles Marina del Rey area. I successfully purchased an existing pizzeria just a few blocks from our home and converted it into a Numero Uno. My wife would manage this location. That location became an immediate and phenomenal success, ranking number two in revenue in the entire chain. Wow! I had discovered an avenue to great wealth with income measured in cash, which would lend itself to better taxation exposure.

My wife's mother, father, and sister lived in Orange County, so I scouted locations in that area for them to manage. Within six months, we opened a location in Tustin and another in Huntington Beach. Shortly after that, I opened three more locations in the Coachella Valley area where we had a second home - two in Palm Springs and one in Palm Desert. Unfortunately, neither of the two Orange County locations was successful, so I sold them both without profit. Of the three Coachella Valley locations, only the Palm Desert location was a success. Unable to sell the other two sites, I closed them, stripped out the furnishings and equipment, put everything in storage, and later sold everything to other restaurant operators, item by item. That left only two operating restaurants, the Marina del Rey location and the Palm Desert restaurant. My wife continued to manage the Marina del Rey location, and we hired a manager for the Palm Desert restaurant under my wife's supervision.

A couple of years later, I accepted an offer of $500,00 from the Numero Uno Corporation for the Marina del Rey location. I also sold my advertising agency and our home in the Marina. We then relocated to the Coachella Valley, and my wife took over the management of the Palm Desert store. The restaurant was only marginally profitable due to what it cost to be a Numero Uno franchisee. In addition to being forced to purchase priority ingredients, including frozen dough, tomato sauce, and salad dressing from the corporate office at inflated fixed prices, we were saddled with a franchise fee of 8 percent and an advertising fee of 3 percent. In the meantime, several other franchisees closed their stores, and the chain's popularity took a nosedive due to mismanagement by the franchisor. It did not take a brain surgeon's intellect to realize that being a Numero Uno franchisee was a losing proposition.

After carefully considering the matter, I decided to disenfranchise unilaterally. I wanted to continue delivering the same product but avoid the time-consuming negotiations and legal costs of a formal disfranchisement process. First and most important was the ability to make pizza with the same slightly sweet crust. We took a dough sample to a local chemist, who identified the ingredient—anise. The only other change we had to make was in the name and the different food item names on the menu.

I elected to rename the restaurant Romano's Trattoria, so we had new menus printed along with a new exterior neon sign for the store. We closed one night as Numero Uno and opened the following morning as Romano's Trattoria. And we did it without notifying the Numero Uno corporate office.

Of course, they later discovered what we had done and advised they were prepared to sue us. After a session or two of negotiation, we settled out of court, with me having to pay $8,000. We continued operating as Romano's Trattoria for several years with a decent profit margin. The only thing I retained of Numero Uno was an etched logo mirror we were presented with when we signed the original franchise agreement. After calculating and weighing investment against income, I concluded that that mirror cost me about $300,000.

LESSON LEARNED

Sometimes, it is easier to ask for forgiveness than ask for permission.

A DEAL WITH MONTY HALL

In the 1970s and 80s, when I had my advertising agency in Los Angeles, I joined the Variety Club, Tent 29 (chapter). A fellow member was Monty Hall, host of the TV program "Let's Make a Deal."

Monty was a notable member, having been named "Chairman for life" due to his lifelong commitment to and support of the Club. But before I expound on my deal with Monty, let me tell you a little about Variety Club.

Variety Club was founded in 1927 by 11 theatre owners and showmen in Pittsburgh, Pennsylvania. Playing cards backstage after a matinee performance at the Sheridan Square Theatre, the men, who informally called their group the Variety Club, heard whimpering from the auditorium. When they investigated, they discovered a one-month-old baby girl to whom her mother had pinned a desperate note: "My name is Catherine. Please help me."

When all efforts by the police and local newspapers failed to locate the parents, the club members decided that they would act as 11 "Godfathers" and underwrite Catherine's support and education. Proud that a distraught mother had entrusted her precious child to them, the club members set out to raise money and obtain goods needed for Catherine's care. The resulting publicity put Catherine's story and Variety on the front pages of newspapers across the United States. Inspired by Catherine's story, many other people wanted to get involved.

One thing led to another, and as a result, today, there are hundreds of Variety Club tents across numerous countries, all devoted to providing help to children in need.

Now, back to my deal with Monty Hall. During a local Los Angeles Variety Club telethon, Monty took time on the air to promote a drawing for a brand new Cadillac El Dorado convertible, which I had arranged to be donated by a client of my agency,

Dixon Cadillac, in Hollywood. Not expecting Dixon Cadillac owner Jack Goodman to contribute the total value of the automobile, I convinced three local television stations to provide Dixn Cadillac with $5,000 worth of free advertising, leaving Dixon's bottom line contribution less than $3,000. To compete in the drawing, entrants paid $100, with the Cadillac valued at $20,000. We ended up with over 500 entrants and over $50,000.

All in all, my efforts in arranging the donation of the Cadillac agency, coupled with Monty's ability to promote the drawing, resulted in a meaningful contribution to our Variety Club Tent 29.

LESSON LEARNED

Finding a way to accomplish the impossible usually requires thinking outside the box and exploring unconventional approaches. This experience underscores the importance of innovation and creativity in problem-solving and encourages us to embrace alternative perspectives.

MY SPECIAL FRIEND, JOE

When I owned and operated my advertising agency, I had a policy of being friendly with my clients but never becoming intimately close because I felt it was in the best interest of our business relationship to maintain an "at arms-length" personal relationship. However, I broke that commitment to one of my clients - Joseph P. Mazzola. My relationship with Joe became "Famiglia." I can't explain it, but there was something about this man that reached the emotional depth of my very being. And, from every indication, while never verbalized, he seemed to find something in me that made him treat me like family. I have often wondered, without conclusion, if our mutual Italian heritage had anything to do with our relationship. In reflecting on our relationship as I write this, I think that Joe, 18 years my senior, at least filled the role of a surrogate uncle to me. Or, maybe it was because he reminded me of my maternal grandfather, Joe, who migrated to the United States from Italy in the early 1900s. I am not sure, and it doesn't matter. Acknowledgment of the importance of our relationship is what matters.

Let me digress for a moment and note that this could be a very long story, but in brevity and focus, I will attempt to keep it at a reasonable length. It is a potentially long story because Joe shared an extraordinary, engaging, and colorful life experience with me as a great storyteller. During our short relationship of not more than ten years, I learned to not only respect this man but to love him. I wept more tears at his funeral than I did for my parents.

Joe was the business manager of Plumbers and Pipefitters U.A. Local 38 in San Francisco, a position he held from 1954 until his death in 1989. The union had established an industry promotion/advertising fund, one of my advertising agency clients, and a resort owned by the Union, Konocti Harbor Inn, located on Clear Lake in Lake County, California.

Joe was a powerful man not only in his industry but also in the politics of San Francisco, particularly on a national level. His ability to deliver votes made him a man to be pursued by politicians. One close associate of Joe's was the infamous Willie Brown, most noted as speaker of the California State Assembly from 1981 to 1995. Willie is but one of many politicians with whom Joe had first-name relationships. San Francisco Mayor Joe Aliota was another, who appointed Joe to three commissions: The San Francisco Housing Authority, the Golden Gate Bridge District, and the Airports Commission. His ability to deliver his union members' votes for Democratic presidential candidates opened doors to many important political figures on a national level as well. For example, he worked hard for and became quite close to Hubert Humphrey when Humphrey ran for president in 1968.

Joe was a master at malapropisms and sprinkled them plentifully without hinting that what he had said was humorous, if not downright laughable. However, it was an endearing part of the man despite its laughableness. His constant use of "blue" language was not so adorable, and he seemed not to note nor care when or where he allowed it to spew forth. He did it often when he was redressing an employee. I recall one occasion when I was sitting in his office, and he called in an employee with whom he had a problem, accusing him of doing something unacceptable. I sat there, embarrassed to be present, while Joe accosted the employee with a string of expletives that would turn the devil's face red. Finally, Joe dismissed the employee with the closing statement: "You must be guilty, or you wouldn't have sat there and let me talk to you the way I did." That was Joe.

Joe also had little concern for the time of day…or night, for that matter. Anytime he had an idea he wanted to discuss, he would pick up the phone. More than once, I was waked in the middle of the night because Joe wanted to tell me something or get my opinion about an idea. He never once found it necessary to apologize for waking me at two or 3 a.m. Just like a kid, he just couldn't wait. That was Joe.

Joe was a self-made man, having grown up as an orphan in Brooklyn, New York. As a young man, he "rode the rails" from coast to coast and escaped or all-too-often endured the "clubbing" of the "bulls" (aggressive lawmen hired by the train companies to keep hobos from hitching rides in the freight train boxcars). Joe was not an educated man, but he was certainly intelligent. His "street smarts" enabled him to rise from an indistinguishable poor orphan boy during the Depression to a compelling and respected person in a major city in the United States and nationally.

As I noted earlier, Joe's vocabulary included many words not recommended for the faint-at-heart. His constant use of some terms seemed so natural that he was unaware of their inappropriateness. However, one story he told me seems to prove that, once in a while, he was aware that his choice of words in the context of the situation was not exactly the best. Joe had just been to the Department of Motor Vehicles to renew his driver's license. After passing the test and walking out of the DMV, he presumably met a nun who was arriving to renew her driver's license. After greeting her with "Hello," Joe said, "Good luck, sister, but watch out 'cause the test is f--king hard to pass." Oops! Sorry sister. Too late. But that was Joe.

Joe owned a ranch and home near Konocti Harbor Inn, and he would occasionally have a few of us guys sleep at the house when we were up at the Inn on business. One night during the winter, with the temperature nearing zero outside, Joe built a fire in a vast fireplace in the living area. Joe meticulously conducted a class on making a fire in a fireplace by methodically and strategically placing the logs. It was an exact science in Joe's mind. He kept piling on logs, one after the other, and we who had gathered around the fireplace had to keep moving back away until finally, we all huddled against the opposite wall, wiping sweat from our brows. Joe had built a really great fire just as he had instructed us during the process…that was Joe.

Joe also was a regular at the track. He loved to "play the ponies," he and his wife, Vera, came very close to a "super duper" dramatic win one day at Golden Gate Fields in Berkeley. Joe placed a pick-six bet and, after all his picks in the first five races had won, his horse in the sixth race came up a nose short in a photo finish. Damn it to hell! That is my explicative. I can, with assurance, imagine Joe's was much more colorful and descriptive. Shortly after Joe's death, Local 38 established the Joseph P. Mazzola Memorial Horse Race at Golden Gate Fields. The race continues to this day and is held annually at Thanksgiving time.

The ranch Joe owned was a walnut tree farm, and he grew Northern California Black walnuts, which are the desirable rootstock for grafting to English walnut stock because they are resistant to soil-borne pests and diseases. Like so many other things he decided to do, Joe became a horticultural expert on walnut farming, from nurturing the important mother tree to irrigation techniques to recognizing the prized paradox rootstock sprouts.

The most intimate and satisfying time I spent with Joe was when he requested that I accompany him to Tasmania. Joe had sold thousands of black walnut seeds to a major onion-growing operation in Tasmania, and conditions of the amount of money to be collected were contingent upon the count of paradox sprouts. The purpose of the trip was to confirm the number qualifying for payment. Following our visit to the fields near the community of Hobart, Tasmania, we took a side trip to Sydney and Melbourne for a few days before returning home. I constantly had to remind Joe to watch out for traffic because motorists were driving on the wrong side of the street. Joe discovered a local race track in Melbourne, so we spent one afternoon placing our bets on the ponies. In one particular race, there was a horse named Vera, which we felt was a good omen in that Joe's wife's name was Vera. Sorry, the prophecy turned out to be a fluke. Joe conducted himself like a curious kid on the trip. That was Joe.

It was Saturday, August 12, 1989. I was doing some "catch-up" paperwork when the phone rang. Earl, Konocit Harbor Inn's manager, was on the line. "Just wanted to let you know Joe was killed this morning." What! That can't be true. No way. But, sadly, it was true. Joe was out on the ranch with a friend, driving in a World War II jeep that he used to roam the steep hills of the ranch. Somehow, the brakes went out, and the jeep started "wheeling downhill" faster and faster. Joe lost control and was thrown out, and the jeep then rolled over, crushing him to death. Suffice it to say…I was stunned into utter disbelief. How could this be? Even at 72, Joe seemed bigger than life…an image of invincibility. But then, that was Joe. Unfortunately, the reality prevailed in this case.

While Joe's death occurred some 27 years ago, as I write this, I still think of him often and occasionally visit with him in my dreams. It is incredible what an impact he has had, and continues to have, on my life. When thinking of him, I remember the saying: "Real friends are family without a birth certificate."

As I mentioned at the beginning of this story, it could have been much longer. However, in brevity, I have simply skimmed over some of the highlights of Joe's life. Hopefully, I have successfully "painted a meaningful character picture" of my friend. To be sure, Joe was much more than the man I have sparingly described here.

LESSON LEARNED

As I have noted in other stories, there are people with whom we come into contact who sometimes play a significant role in our lives, as is the case with my friend Joe, a role that lives on beyond death.

IF A BRICK FALLS FROM THE SKY, WHAT NEXT?

In the 1970s and '80s, when I operated an advertising agency in Beverly Hills, I had to make many decisions—some relatively easy and others quite complex. One of the more difficult decisions I had to make was to terminate the employment of an associate with whom I had a cordial relationship and, to my knowledge, had done nothing to warrant his termination. The employee was Jon, and his position was assistant account executive on the agency's PIP (Postal Instant Press) account.

One day, the PIP account executive to whom Jon reported came to me and advised me that the president of PIP told her he did not want Jon to accompany her on future appointments. He also clarified that he didn't want Jon working on the account in any capacity whatsoever. He was emphatic about his decision but declined to explain. My first thought was to contact the client and ask why he had delivered this ultimatum. My second thought, however, was confirmation that this would not be in the best interest of our retaining PIP as an important client. While I did not understand why the client had decided, it was not my prerogative to interrogate him on the decision. In other words, he was the client, and it was in our best interest to address his wishes, whatever the reason. Otherwise, he could easily decide it was time for an agency review, and we could lose an important client over the refusal to adapt to his decision.

Jon's only responsibility at the agency was to assist with the details of servicing the PIP account. No other position was available at our firm if he were prohibited from working on the account. Therefore, I had to terminate Jon's employment. I invited Jon to join me for lunch at the Friars Club, where I was a member. We enjoyed small talk over the meal, and then came the dreaded moment when I had to come clean. I explained to Jon the circumstances that forced me to make the decision and expressed my disappointment in having to make it. While it impacted Jon with a particular surprise, he handled the situation calmly and clearly. As we got ready to get up from the table, I told Jon, "When a brick falls out of the sky and hits you on the head, don't cry, but pick it up and ask yourself what you can build with it."

I am pleased to know that Jon didn't waste any time crying over falling bricks but did go on to build a fulfilling career in law enforcement and establish a family with the loving, nurturing capacity of an exceptional husband and parent.

Jon and I lost contact with each other after he left the agency, and it was not until some thirty years later that we reconnected. Today, Jon and I correspond regularly. He is now retired and enjoying the good life of a husband, father, and grandfather. I can honestly say that even though we are miles apart – he is in Tennessee, and I am in California – Jon is one of my best friends. He is a genuine man who can share personal experiences with me and offer me words of optimism and encouragement when appropriate.

I don't think my sage advice about 'falling bricks' really had anything to do with Jon's ability to overcome adversity. I am confident that he would have accomplished the things he did in his life had I not offered one word of advice.

LESSON LEARNED

Along with authority comes responsibility. Sometimes, this responsibility forces one to make distasteful and difficult decisions.

WHEN A WORK OF ART TAKES CENTER STAGE

In the early-to-mid 1980s, I purchased a work of art from a business associate who was also a personal friend. The result was an early effort by the amateur artist whose day job was as an account executive for a local radio station assigned to work with the media buying department of my advertising agency.

The account executive/artist had a showing one evening at a local bank branch, and I, the media buyers from my agency, and others attended the event as a show of support for our friend. With no previous intent to purchase, I found one piece, a collage, appealing. So, I bought it for the price of $800. Not being an art collector, this was an unusual purchase for me, but it conveyed a unique, meaningful, undefined, pleasing message. I proudly displayed it in the living room of our home and soon discovered that visitors also admired and found something special in the collage. The fact that others shared my appreciation gave me an extra sense of contentment with the art piece, granting me a feeling that my unlearned taste in art was, after all, artistically valid. Even though we moved several times since making the art purchase, I always found a prominent place to display the collage for others to see and appreciate.

Years passed, and the once-unknown artist's talent began to bloom like a well-tended garden. The artist's name echoed through galleries, art magazines, and conversations among the art elite. The unique style, the very one that had drawn me to make the purchase, had become the artist's signature and gave rise to fame as a visionary talent. In addition, this artist has an impressive list of private collectors, including Maya Angelou, Bill Russell, Oprah Winfrey, Ron and Charlayne Hunter-Gaultt, Gordon Parks, and Maria Gibbs.

She was chosen as one of six artists honored by the Museum of African Art for contributions to contemporary art, named the official artist for the 1987 Los Angeles Marathon, selected to design the International Tennis Trophy and Medal for the 1984

Summer Olympics, and won the Museum of Science and Industry's 1984 Black Creativity Juried Art Show for her work, *Waiting Room*. The artist also participated in the design of the presidential seal for former President Bill Clinton's inaugural.

Television and film personality Oprah Winfrey commissioned the artist to do a series of paintings and lithographs based on Winfrey's award-winning mini-series, *The Women of Brewster Place*.

Sometime in the early 2000s, my son, Justin, told me that while browsing the internet, he discovered that the collage I owned was on display at the Smithsonian Museum in Washington, D. C. How could that be? Long story short, I learned that museum personnel had seen a photo of the piece and contacted the artist requesting to display it. Even though the artist knew I had the work and knew how to contact me, they instead elected to duplicate it.

My initial reaction was one of outrage. How dare a one-time friend do that? I felt betrayed and cheated because my art piece could now fetch thousands of dollars. I considered litigating the matter with anticipation that I would prevail. After researching, however, I found that duplicating an original work sold may be void of high ethical standards. However, it is not illegal because, as I learned, unless the artist has given written copyright ownership of a piece of art to the buyer, the copyright remains with the creator. When you buy an original painting, you purchase the physical object to have and enjoy. In most circumstances, you own only the artwork, not its copyright.

LESSON LEARNED

This scenario reminds me of what Charles R. Swindoll noted: "Life is 10% what happens to you and 90% how you react to it." While I initially felt betrayed and cheated, I later saw the situation as a tribute to the magic of discovery and a testament to the power of believing in the unseen potential of others.

T-Time Becomes A Hole-In-One

In the mid-1990s, I suddenly found I had no business, job, or income. I was devastated. Growing up on a farm in southern Missouri, I had worked consistently since I was about 12. I even held part-time jobs during my undergraduate college years and worked during the summers as a construction worker to pay for my education. I was 59 years old, and the prospect of nothing to do and no income at my age was beyond my ability to grasp with any sense of confidence. I panicked. Where do I go from here? My panic quadrupled. I had a wife and a 5-year-old son to provide for. With no income, we would surely lose our home and the way of life to which we had become accustomed.

As luck would have it, we inherited a small amount of money within weeks – enough to pay our essential bills for about six or eight months. After finally conquering my panic (or at least keeping it from devouring my every thought from the time I awoke in the morning 'til I fell asleep at night with the aid of sleeping pills), I sat down with my wife. I told her I needed to "do nothing" for six months and gain enough composure to plan for an economic and emotional recovery. Being the devout wife she is, she understood and agreed with my decision.

Day after day, I would sit in my recliner and ponder the future. What can I do to put our lives back together?

My first approach was to try my hand at writing children's books. So, I enrolled in a correspondence course and began writing. While I found this to be an enjoyable endeavor, I soon realized that becoming a published author was not going to be an easy task, and more importantly, even if I were to become successful as a writer and earn an income from it, the amount of revenue was questionable. The time it would take to realize any significant money would, in all probability, be much longer than the time I was afforded to start bringing in the funds we would need to survive. So, back to my recliner and more contemplation about the future.

This was during the pre-internet era when big money was being made by operating 900 number pay-per-call businesses. I had an acquaintance making an excellent income running such a business, so I started considering how to create a 900-number business. After viewing several advice-line topics, I launched a pay-for-call operation giving men tips on how to pick up women. I wrote a script, recorded it, and ran inexpensive print ads targeting the young male demographic. I waited for the calls to roll in, but they didn't happen. Back to the drawing board, or rather the recliner.

At this point, I asked myself two critical questions: Where am I, and what is it that I know how to do? Answer to the first question: Palm Springs, California, is a resort community that has earned the title Golf Capital of the World. Answer to the second question: Create and produce radio and television commercials and programs as I had done when I operated my advertising firm. So, why not create a local television program that promotes local public-play golf courses to visiting golfers? It hadn't been done, but that was no reason not to do it. That was the embryo of an idea from which I developed a 30-minute program featuring five 5-minute segments showing the program's host playing a couple of holes with the club pro from five golf clubs. The five golf clubs featured on the program paid for the TV exposure. That left me with another three minutes to fill with 30-second commercials. I sold these to local advertisers looking to reach visiting tourist golfers. It was a revenue-driven concept from the program beginning of the program sign-off. My income would be the margin between what I charged the golf courses and advertisers to be on the program, what I had to pay for TV airtime, production and editing, and the host's charges.

Okay, I had what I thought was a good idea, but there was one huge problem. I am not a golfer and didn't know the game's terminology. I didn't know a "hook" from a "slice" or a "birdie" from a "bogey." What to do? This being a time before there was a computer with Google in every home, I headed for the library and began reading every golf book I could find. I also started quizzing some of my friends and family members who did "hit the greens."

The first T-Time program hit the air in 1997 with a daily TV airing schedule in early fringe time. I hired a local long-driving freelance golfer to host the program, who quickly became a local celebrity. Later, after meeting Tommy Jacobs, an American Senior PGA golfer who owned and operated a local golf club, I convinced him to take over the program host duties. This gave the program added credentials. Tommy was well-known and respected as a winning professional golfer, with seven professional wins to his credit, including the 1964 Bob Hope Classic (known back then as the Palm Springs Golf Classic.) Tommy continued as the host of T-Time 'til we took it off the air in 2007.

The answers to two simple self-imposed questions while sitting in my recliner created a source of income for me and my family for an entire decade. Even though I still do not pick up the "sticks," I will contend that I hit a "hole in one" with T-Time.

LESSON LEARNED

Unless you are an accomplished intuitive decision-maker, devote sufficient time to sorting out the essential details of an idea before coming to a decision.

MOBSTER ATTORNEY ELECTED MAYOR

In the early 1970s, I lived in Las Vegas for a few years and produced/directed a local TV program featuring high-end residential real estate for sale. I came up with the idea that a 2-minute segment within the program featuring Oscar Goodman, the mayor of Las Vegas, making a positive statement about the benefits of living in Las Vegas would enhance the program. After stating the purpose, I contacted Oscar's office and requested a meeting with the mayor. Fortunately, my request was honored, and a few days later, we met, and he agreed with my proposal. The mayor was noted for being a jovial fellow and made no secret about his favorite adult beverage, gin martinis. Consumption of his beverage of choice was a daily routine multiple times per day. He even had his own personal recipe for his martinis - no vermouth and, instead of the typical olive, a jalapeno for garnish. And he likes them shaken instead of stirred.

Knowing the mayor's openly celebrated fondness for his martinis, I asked him if he would object if I titled his segment of the TV program "A Martini Moment with the Mayor." Not only did he not object, but he laughed and said that was a very appropriate title.

While the mayor and I did not become buddy-buddy friends, we did develop a mutually respectful and professional association. As a result, my wife and I were invited to the mayor's victory party following his third term reelection in 2007, which was his last due to a three-term limit. Not to worry, though, he arranged for his wife, Carolyn, to be elected mayor following his departure. She remains mayor now, in 2023. That is a typical tactic of Oscar, who, in earlier years, displayed his unique talent as a successful trial attorney in Las Vegas. (More about that later).

In keeping with his somewhat unique approach to life, Oscar, while in office, is reported to have a clause in the contract with any movie or TV show production to be filmed in Las Vegas that called for a part in the production for Oscar. Fact or fiction, the mayor did appear in several productions, including the top-rated Scorsese movie Casino.

Now, at the heart of this story is Oscar Goodman's career as an attorney. Not just your ordinary attorney but a Mob Attorney. As a young lawyer, Oscar successfully represented high-profile mobsters during the mafia's tenure as casino operators and skimmers in Las Vegas. He defended the most infamous members of organized crime in the United States. Men like Meyer Lansky, Lefty Rosenthal, Nicky Scarfo, and Anthony Spilotro. As their lawyer, he stood by them and kept them out of prison for as long as possible. And with every successful case, his reputation grew. His most dramatic courtroom victory was when he obtained a Not-guilty verdict for the El Paso drug kingpin, Jimmy Chagra. While he had no problem associating with criminals professionally, Oscar maintained a strict policy of never socializing with any of them.

Oscar was also the moving force behind creating the Las Vegas Mob Museum, which opened in 2014 and is officially named the National Museum of Organized Crime and Law Enforcement. It is located in downtown Las Vegas in the 1933-constructed Federal Courthouse, left empty upon completion of a new courthouse. The old courthouse was scheduled to be torn down, but at Oscar's urging, city officials expressed an interest in purchasing the building. In 2002, the feds sold the building to the City of Las Vegas for $1, stipulating that it be preserved and used as a cultural center. The museum has become a must-visit destination in Las Vegas, attracting 400,000 visitors annually, employing 150 people and scores of dedicated volunteers.

LESSON LEARNED

This story highlights the power of good governance and its impact on the community. A person's past association with criminals within a community need not deter them from later dedicating themselves to public service and bringing unique perspectives and approaches to addressing that community's needs.

"THE EVENING SEASON OF A STORIED LIFE."

"Even the seasons form a great circle in their changing and always come back to where they were. A person's life is a circle from childhood to childhood, and so it is in everything where power moves."

—Black Elk

And now, we come to the Evening Season of my Life, and there are stories worth telling here, too.

A Little White Bundle Of Love

The month was February…, and the year was 2008. It was after dark, and we had just come through the gate to the community where we lived in the northeastern area of Las Vegas. Suddenly and unexpectedly, the lights of the car caught the sight of a small white animal running in the street ahead of us. I pointed it out to my wife, and neither she nor I could tell if it was a cat, a rabbit, or a little dog. Regardless of what it was, the little thing appeared to be running scared, so we decided we needed to rescue it if possible.

At last, we determined the little white creature to be a tiny dog, but we could never quite catch up with it. It managed to elude us as we continued winding down different streets within the community. Finally, we gave up and went to our apartment. I kept waking up during the night wondering what would become of this little animal who seemed so lost and scared. I couldn't get its fate off my mind.

The following day, I had an appointment to be away from home. Upon returning, I decided to drive around our community with the chance that I might see that little white dog that had so successfully thwarted our attempts to catch up with it the evening before. After driving for only a few minutes, I spotted the little dog hiding under a staircase not far from our apartment. I stopped the car and called my wife, Debra, on my cell. I told her where I was, and she dropped whatever she was doing and rushed to find us…me still in the car and the little dog under the stairs. Debra got down on her hands and knees and slowly maneuvered her way within reach of the frightened little thing. She coaxed the little dog to lie still so she could get hold of her. Success! We finally had made our rescue. Now what?

Here, I will digress briefly to explain. About three weeks earlier, we had to "put down" our 15-year-old Springer Spaniel, Rummy. It was a tearful and painful experience, and because of the "hurt, " Debra and I had determined that we would

160

not get another dog, at least for some time, so we wouldn't have to face a similar, difficult time with another pet.

The first thing we did was take the little dog, which was a female, to a local veterinarian to determine her health. After a thorough examination, she was declared healthy but dehydrated and needed nourishment. The vet estimated her age to be six weeks, and her breed is a mix of Maltese and Poodle – a Maltipoo. The second thing we did was attempt to locate the owner before we could become attached. We posted "lost and found" notices throughout our community and notified the office of our find in case anyone might be looking for a little, lost, white doggie. After over a week, no one came forward to claim our discovery. So we, then and there, adopted the little white dog to be a new member of our household. Debra decided Marshmellow would be an appropriate name for her. Yes, I know, the word should be spelled marshmallow, but I made an error in first scribing her name and later defended my mistake by declaring I had misspelled her name on purpose because she was so "mellow."

At first, Marshmellow wouldn't eat or even drink. At the vet's suggestion, we purchased Pedialyte and baby food. While she did drink small amounts of Pedialyte, she still refused to eat, so I would put some baby food on my finger and dab some on her nose, which she would then lick off. Little by little, she came around and started eating and drinking as a healthy puppy should.

A humorous incident is that, after a few days with us, Marshmellow climbed upon the pillow and rested right next to Debra's head. She then proceeded to pee on Debra's head...and from that moment on, she was declared a member of our household. Debra laughingly accepted the pee-pee episode as a testament to committed motherhood.

Fast forward some seven years. Today, Marshmellow, Debra, and I reside in the Orange County area of Southern California (Ladera Ranch) after living in Boston for four years (2008 to 2012). Marshmellow has flown coast-to-coast twice without incident and has become a notable resident of the 55+ community in which we live. Many of our neighbors know her name but do not recall our names. She loves to ride in the car with us everywhere we go, and we feel guilty when she can't join us. We often seek out local cafes and restaurants with outside patio seating so she can join us for a meal. She also has become a bed partner and will usually lie on her back by my thigh so I can rub her belly until she falls asleep. Have we become obsessed pet parents? No question about it. This little white bundle of love has given us contentment and joy that only "man's best friend" can provide. She is, however, much more than a friend….Marshmellow is family!

LESSON LEARNED

Sometimes in our lives, we don't make the decisions….instead, they are made for us.

AMERICAN GRANDPA...A CHERISHED BADGE OF HONOR

I returned to the classroom in 2009 after receiving my bachelor of arts degree in speech and drama from the University of Missouri in 1958 – over a half-century later. This time, I pursued a master's degree in leadership at Northeastern University in Boston. I attended classes both on campus and online. I must admit that returning to school at the age of 75 was an experience fraught with nagging anxiety and concern. Not only were my classmates much younger than me, most in their early or mid-twenties, but also all of my instructors were the age of my older children. Initially, I felt like the proverbial "fish out of water." Thankfully, my anxiety and concern soon dissipated as I found that while I stood out as "different" from the typical student, I was accepted without prejudice. Not only was I welcomed by this acceptance, but it also stimulated my desire to prove that "an old dog can learn new tricks" along with the young pups.

I remember one group project where I was one of four members charged with making a class presentation. The other three group members were young men in their early twenties – about one-fourth my age. All young enough to be my grandsons. As a group, we had several out-of-class on-campus meetings to prepare for our presentation. Not only was I unconditionally accepted by the others as an essential member of the group, but I also found that my three classmates genuinely respected my input and creative ideas for our presentation. It was an enjoyable experience and one that inspired me. Ours was one of several other groups in the class assigned to make presentations, and part of the exercise was to name our group. I suggested calling our group "Three Hunks and a Dinosaur." My proposed group name was adopted, and when we announced it in class before making our presentation, we were greeted with warm laughter and applause. This, quite effectively, set the stage for a successful production. It was a "sick" presentation in today's youth's vocabulary.

163

Unlike my growing-up years in a Southern Missouri single-dimensioned, rural community of "redneck" Waspish Caucasians of European descent, and even unlike my years as a student at Mizzou back in the 1950s where the vast majority of students were residents of the state and white, the student body make-up at Northeastern University was quite diverse, with many of my classmates being, not only much younger than I but also foreign students. With gratitude, I found that many students and I quickly related to each other, especially several Asian students. I suspect this was due, in large part, to the Asian, and especially the Chinese, tradition of "filial piety," which emphasizes the value of total respect for the family, especially the elders. Confucius advocated this respect for elders, a famous Chinese philosopher, and most Chinese families choose to continue these ancient principles today.

In particular, one young female student from China and I developed a connectedness with acknowledged respect for each other. I shared three on-campus classes with this young lady, who had chosen to be known by an Americanized name, Jenny. Her Chinese name is Pan Pan Liu. One day after class, Jenny leaned over and asked me a question. "May I adopt you as my American grandpa?" she queried. I was surprised by Jenny's request and appropriately pleased and quickly responded, "Indeed you may; I am delighted that you would ask." I embraced this cross-cultural acceptance with a feeling I find challenging to explain. However, if asked to describe my experience, I would suggest two words – honored and accepted. We exchanged personal e-mail addresses and engaged in ongoing personal communication outside of classes.

Upon completion of her master's studies in 2011, Jenny prepared to return to her home in China, which, according to her, is a small town, albeit with a population that exceeds 1 million. It is not very small compared to my hometown, with a population of 2,000. The primary industry in her hometown of Liuyang is the manufacture of fireworks; that is the business in which her family works – they own a small company, according to Jenny.

Jenny's fiancé, Chen, came to Boston to accompany her home, and before they left, they hosted me at a luncheon at Jenny's favorite Chinese restaurant in Boston. It was a bitter-sweet occasion, and while I was pleased that Jenny had completed her studies with outstanding achievement, it also meant that we probably would not see each other again.

It has now been five years since Jenny and I saw each other. However, we have kept in contact via e-mail and a couple of phone calls. Jenny has embarked on a career in banking. I was invited to the wedding when she and Chen married about two years ago. While I could not attend, I was delighted to receive pictures of the wedding and reception. Jenny was a beautiful bride. They recently moved into a new home and are happily expecting their first child. In my most recent e-mail from Jenny, she told me that she and Chen planned to give their child an Americanized nickname and a formal Chinese name. She asked permission to give their child, should it be a boy, the name "Wayne." Once again, I felt honored and, with haste, assured Jenny they do, indeed, have my permission and blessing.

My wife and I are invited to be guests in Jenny and Chen's home, and they are in ours. While I will probably never see Jenny again, I am pleased to continue our "across-the-globe" friendship and know that my life has been enriched by knowing her.

LESSON LEARNED

People can learn a lot by not being confined to the cultural values and mores under which they are born and raised. Many benefits can be derived from keeping an open mind of acceptance.

WHAT'S RIGHT IS RIGHT, AND WHAT'S WRONG IS WRONG

This will not be one of my longer stories, but the lesson learned is important. At the time, we were living in a 55-plus apartment complex in Ladera Ranch, a community in Orange County, California. One morning, as I was walking to our car in the apartment complex parking lot, I noticed a note on the ground paper-clipped to a ten-dollar bill. I thought, "Oh, lucky me, I now have ten extra bucks to spend. Maybe I'll buy myself a bottle of Petite Sirah."

I picked up the note with the attached ten-dollar bill and, reading the message, found it to be a grocery shopping list. And it is a short list because ten dollars will only buy a few groceries nowadays. As I was on the road to perform whatever errands I had on my agenda for the day, I began to have second thoughts about my newfound fortune. I started to question why I considered the matter "Finders, Keepers, Losers, Weepers." Somehow, it just didn't sit well with me as I pondered how I might, instead of keeping the ten dollars, go about trying to find the person who lost it. After a while, it came to me: there is a bulletin board in the mail room at our apartment complex. I will remove the ten-dollar bill and post the grocery list note, "I found this grocery list a few days ago in the parking lot, and if you can tell me what was attached to it, please call me." I included my name and phone number.

A Few days later, I received a phone call from a lady who lived in our apartment complex. She told me precisely what was attached to the note, so I felt confident I had located the person who had lost the money and the message. The caller gave me her apartment number, and I immediately returned the ten dollars to her. I was pleased that my search for the owner was successful. But that is not all that pleased me. My neighbor told me that the grocery list and money belonged to a shut-in elderly lady-friend who also lived in the apartment complex and that she was on her way to pick up the necessary food items for her friend when she lost both the note and the money. Suddenly, my pleasure at finding the owner of the message and money took a giant leap forward. I had done the right thing, and besides giving me pleasure, I was now confident that I had undoubtedly relieved two of my neighbors from their worry and displeasure at having lost the money.

LESSON LEARNED

There is much more pleasure and contentment in knowing that you have done what is right, even though you could have done the opposite. Doing what is right is undoubtedly suitable and pleasurable, and doing what is wrong is no way to find either pleasure or contentment.

THE CASE OF A CONFUSED COBB SALAD

During my late wife's ongoing battle with cancer, she was admitted for treatment at M.D. Anderson's Cancer Center in Houston, Texas, about a four-hour drive from our home in a suburb of Austin, Texas. We often made trips for a few days' stay in Houston for her treatment. On the way, we would stop about midway to and from Houston for a brief rest and often a meal at one of a well-known national chain of restaurants.

On one particular trip home, we stopped for lunch, and I selected a favorite of mine, a Cobb salad. The young lady serving us took our order, and my wife's order arrived promptly. However, my order took an extra long time to arrive finally. And when it did, the plate held a peculiar mix of ingredients resembling neither a Cobb salad nor any recognizable dish.

Confused and agitated, I caught the eye of the manager and motioned for her to come to our table. I showed her the plate before me and queried if the plate before me looked like a Cobb salad. She immediately agreed with my confusion and quickly advised that my lunch would be comped, then turned and walked into the kitchen. Soon afterward, our young server approached our table, visibly stressed, apologizing and saying this was only her third day on the job. While I felt she should have admitted she did not know how to prepare a Cobb salad, I also understood her immature reluctance to do so, especially given what might not be a compassionate understanding management style.

In assessing the unfolding scenario, I found that my attitude switched from agitation to empathy. Empathy for the young server who undoubtedly had not received the appropriate training before being thrust into an unprepared serving position. The next opportunity, I motioned for our young server to come to our table. She approached with trepidation, anticipating, I presume, that I was prepared to lash out at her for such ineptitude. As she came close, I looked her in the eyes and said: "I do not blame you for the disastrous situation regarding my order. Not at all! I blame management for not preparing you with the proper training so that you could perform with knowledge and confidence." She was greatly relieved by what I had said to her. With pleasant well-wishes for a successful and happy future, I handed her a $10 bill. With visible amazement, she, with tears welling up in her eyes, thanked me for my generosity, turned, and walked into the kitchen, but not before looking back at us with a smile and friendly wave.

As my wife and I left the restaurant, I couldn't help but feel contentment. In a simple act of compassion and understanding, I managed to turn an unfortunate dining experience into a heartfelt lesson of empathy and growth. And so, the tale of a cob salad mishap turned into a story of kindness, leaving both our server and me with a memory that could stay with us for years.

LESSON LEARNED

Before jumping to a conclusion when something goes wrong and quickly placing blame, take time to understand the situation's circumstances so you can properly evaluate the cause and make decisions based on fact. What first may seem worthy of anger can turn into a pleasant learning experience.

OH, LOOK...THERE'S A BABY ONE!

During the last couple of years of my wife Debra's life, one event always brought her much energy and delight while battling to survive the torturing effects of her illness. That was observing deer in our backyard through her bedroom window. The sight of deer, be it one, two, or several, seemed to mesmerize her. I would help her out of bed, and she would sit in her wheelchair at the window until the last deer disappeared into the trees and bushes. This was incredibly joyful, especially when a baby deer appeared in the group.

At this time, we lived in a 55-plus community. In Georgetown, Texas, a community of homes nestled in a natural setting of trees and shrubs is a natural habitat for deer and many other creatures of nature. Fortunately, our house backed onto such an area, mere feet from across our backyard lawn. Deer nestled in the trees and bushes often would venture into our backyard at dusk. To encourage them to venture into our yard, I purchased corn and spread it on the lawn where they could nibble it from the grass. This became a daily routine for me when deer became active. My routine became a calling card for the deer, and often, they would show up before I disbursed the corn and wait patiently for me to complete the feeding gesture. This routine also became a time of purity and excitement for Debra.

Debra also received at-home physical therapy twice a week during this time. She and her therapist became more than just a professional and a patient. They became friends with Debra, always looking forward to Michael's visits. The two shared gifts during the holiday season. Their sessions included a lot of conversation dealing with many facets of life, particularly their own lives. While they shared and agreed on many of life's adventures, there was one subject upon which they unwaveringly disagreed - their fondness for deer. While Debra saw deer as something to view and admire, Michael viewed deer as a food source. As a bow-and-arrow hunter, his focus was quite the opposite of Debra's.

Fortunately, this disagreement did not harm or diminish the shared value of their relationship.

I observed a spiritually illuminated alignment between the deer's and Debra's lives. Deer are highly adaptable creatures, capable of thriving in various environments. They possess acute senses and are always alert to their surroundings. From deer, we can learn the importance of adapting to life's changes and challenges while maintaining a heightened awareness of our environment and its opportunities or dangers. This alignment did exist and helped my wife deal with her challenges.

While Debra's illness prohibited us from engaging in the many social activities available in our community, her ability to observe and relish her time with the deer in our backyard made up for the loss. While I no longer live in the community and do not often see deer, the memory of Debra's end-of-life experience with deer has given me a before-unknown appreciation of this animal, plus a new and meaningful jubilation with my fond memories of Debra and her graceful deer.

LESSON LEARNED

Deer are messengers or symbols of spiritual guidance. Observing a deer or a group of deer can be seen as a sign or message from the spiritual realm. It may encourage us to pay attention to our spiritual journey, seek guidance, or reflect on the universe's messages.

LUNA, LUCILLE, ARIELLE, THEN BACK TO LUNA

When my little Marshmellow (*incorrectly spelled on purpose*) passed over the Rainbow Bridge in early 2022, I knew I could never replace her. However, I was also aware of how important it is for me to have a little companion to love me and for me to love. So, I posted a note on my neighborhood Facebook page asking for assistance finding a new furry companion. I was overwhelmed by the many people who stepped forward to help me. When I successfully rescued another little Maltipoo, I posted a picture along with a thank you to all and a brief description of my newly found fur baby.

"As many of you here know, about a month ago, I lost my little loveable Marshmellow as she passed over the Rainbow Bridge after bringing me joy and love for 14 years. Many of you heeded my request for assistance in finding another companion. And for the many of you who responded with caring and love, I thank you."

About ten days ago, I was successful in my desire to rescue and adopt another little Maltipoo girl. Here is an update on that little Maltipoo.

I was told her name was Lucille. This name did not fit her personality, so I renamed her Arielle, a Hebrew word meaning *lioness of God*. After receiving her recorded medical history, I found that her name was not Lucille but Luna (in Hebrew, a name meaning "dweller.") Also, Luna is a name that indicates a gift of gab - the ability to persuade others effortlessly. Those with the name are expressive, optimistic, outgoing, and inspiring. Charming and cheerful, they are the life of the party for any social event. This description is a perfect fit for my little girl. So, I have decided to abandon naming her Arielle and keep her name Luna. Let me explain why.

I have learned that at the age of 8 weeks and weighing just 1.75 lbs. Luna was diagnosed with coccidiosis, an intestinal tract infection caused by a single-celled organism (protozoa) called coccidia. Coccidiosis causes diarrhea, dehydration, abdominal distress, and vomiting. However, in puppies and debilitated adult dogs, coccidiosis may cause severe watery diarrhea, dehydration, abdominal pain, and vomiting. In extreme cases, death may occur. In reviewing the veterinarian's report, Luna's condition was severe, and she was literally at death's door. Unfortunately, her pet parents could not pay for treatment, so they had to abandon her and leave her with the veterinarian.

Thank goodness, and with much thankfulness, the veterinarian gave this little puppy a long-shot chance for survival. She spent days in the ICU dealing with life-threatening conditions and underwent various tests and treatments, including a blood transfusion and medications. Thanks to the veterinarian's diligent, prompt, and caring response and other unknown forces of spiritual intervention, Luna made it and was later put up for adoption. When I learned of her being available for adoption, I applied and, gratefully, was selected to give her a loving, forever home."

LESSON LEARNED

Names do have meanings! After giving the situation much thought, I have concluded that it was not Lucille or Arielle who fought so hard in that hospital to survive; it was Luna. Therefore, my little sweetheart's name will appropriately remain Luna.

A Message Of Burning Candles And Music

O n October 7, 2022, my son Justin and daughter-in-law Ashley blessed me with a grandson, Asher Judah. Now, six months later, I am amazed and joyful with how wonderfully and lovingly Justin and Ashley have embraced their role of parenthood. This little boy has become, as it should be, the central purpose of their reason for being. While both Justin and Ashley have been caring, responsible individuals, the birth of their son has multiplied their caring and love a hundred times over. Their attention to Asher's many infancy needs establishes the foundation for him to grow and mature into a man with many outstandingly good character qualities of astute significance.

Ashley and Justin are adept at nourishing Asher's need for a well-adapted growth pattern, including healthy nourishment, good hygiene, spiritual development, and a curious mind. Justin's constant attention to the daddy-son physical relationship and Ashely's mommy-reading-time every day, especially at bedtime, preparing for a night of calm and rest, is evidenced by Asher's delight and engagement in the activities.

While I am not Jewish, my late wife, Debra, was. Having no solid religious belief, I welcomely accept and respect the many tenets of the Jewish faith. I learned much through osmosis as I accompanied Debra to Friday night services in the synagogue and celebrated the many Jewish holidays throughout the years. Our son, Justin, was reared as a Jew and was bar mitzvahed as a teenager, the traditional Jewish ceremony that signifies a young male youth has reached the age of maturity and has become responsible for his actions. Ashley, too, is non-Jewish but, as do I, embraces Judaism with expectations of converting. The decision to rear Asher as a Jew is a forgone conclusion made mutually by both Justin and Ashley.

174

Of the many aspects of Asher's young exposure to the various principles of life as a child of loving and responsible parents, his early reactions to some of the traditional at-home Jewish family traditions are not only pleasurable to witness but also give reason to believe that he, even at this very early stage of life, is inspired by the specifics of ceremony such as his keen attention to burning candles and his visible physical harmony with the music. Asher's mommy and daddy are pleased to be witnesses to their son's reactions. They feel incredibly blessed, as do I, to have such a child of awareness who seems to appreciate the beauty and significance of the Jewish faith at this very early stage in life. They know and understand, however, that it is up to them to nurture Asher's love for the traditions and make sure they are an ongoing important part of his way of living.

LESSON REMEMBERED, NOT LEARNED.

Mothers and fathers need to embrace and nurture the roles and responsibilities of parenthood. It is also essential to be intentional and proactive in encouraging a child's interests and curiosity to help them grow into well-rounded individuals with good character qualities.

LEARNING TO LIVE WITH SEVERE HEARTACHE

This will be one of my shortest stories. Not because it is not important but because it is painful to write. This story is about the deaths of two of my children: My eldest daughter, Deborah Lynn, and my eldest son, Michael Wayne. I have hesitated about and postponed the writing of this story, but not writing it would be ignoring the two most shattering events in my life – events that have affected me more than any other. I can attest, without hesitation, that their deaths tore at my heart at the time and continue, to this day, to rip away at it.

Our thirty-fourth president, Dwight D. Eisenhower, accurately described the effects of a child's death. After the death of his son Doud, Eisenhower proclaimed, "There's no tragedy in life like the death of a child. Things never get back to the way they were." Indeed, they do not. However, I understand that life must go on. And it does. It just is never the same as before. It does not mean that you forget about things. It just means you have no alternative but to accept what has happened and need to continue living with the knowledge that you will never be free of the pain of your loss.

My daughter came to the end of her life thirty-eight years ago at the age of 23, and my son left us two years ago at 55, neither having the opportunity to live a fulfilled life of happiness. That is what saddens me the most.

I will not go into details surrounding either of their deaths, for it will serve no purpose by telling but would, however, make the writing much more painful.

I often hear talk about the need for closure. However, I don't like the word. It comes from the Latin word Clausura, meaning a finish or conclusion. I do not desire a "finish" or "conclusion" because even though my son and my daughter are no longer with me, their life's special meaning and purpose have not been finished or concluded. Their lives continue to live on within me.

I grieve the loss of my son and my daughter. That grief will continue until the day I die. The following are not my words, but they express my feelings ideally in describing what grief means to me. "Grief is a mirror that we hold up as it reflects our loss to us. We learn to live with the loss and even smile again, but it doesn't go away. As long as we live, we never bring the grief over death to a complete close. There will always be a reflection of loss gazing back at us in the looking glass."

LESSON LEARNED

You must find the strength to carry on with your life even though when tragedy strikes, that life can seem to have been reduced to smoldering ashes.

AN EXPERIENCE OF FEAR, HOPE, AND LOVE

The year is 2023. As I sit here thinking about the often lonely life I now live, I cannot help but feel overwhelmed at times by that dreadful sense of emptiness since my wife Debra's passing two years ago. Our marriage was a second marriage, lasting over 40 beautiful years. We both realized from the moment we first met in 1977 at the Santa Anita Race Track that we were meant to share our special love for a lifetime. We read our vows and tied the matrimonial knot on May 3, 1980.

Sadly, in early November of 2018, our world took a horrible upside-down collapse. That is when Debra underwent an endoscopy and was diagnosed with esophageal cancer. I will never forget when the nurse came back with the results. She said, "The doctor thinks Debra has a malignant tumor and wants her to see an oncologist." My heart took a nose dive and sank to the soles of my feet. I felt as if I had been hit in the chest with a giant wrecking ball. I worked hard to contain my immense fear and feebly attempted to give Debra a reason to be optimistic. I experienced a more devastating and heart-wrenching fear when the oncologist confirmed the gastroenterologist's findings and advised us to prepare for a challenging future of the worst kind.

It was a tough road, and chemo treatments were highly harsh on Debra's body. Her treatment was interrupted during the COVID-19 pandemic, requiring us to remain isolated in our home for over a year. When we were finally comfortable going outside again, we hoped to resume her treatment at the renowned MD Anderson Cancer Center in Houston, Texas. Still, unfortunately, Debra was too weak to start again. She had to undergo several surgeries and spent much time in and out of hospitals and recovery centers. While our love affair had always been intense, actually becoming even stronger during some very trying and worrisome times during our marriage, I can honestly say that my love for Debra was never greater than while caring for her and watching her nearly three-year brave battle to survive and beat the dreaded "Big C." She fought hard, and we held out hope, but eventually, she succumbed in 2021 to the disease. That did not just break my heart but tore it to shreds.

After Debra's passing, life has been somewhat difficult, and I still struggle to cope with her loss. However, I am lucky to have our son Justin and his wife Ashley in my life. Justin was born to us despite my original desire to father no more children with Debra because of the tragic death of my oldest daughter from my first marriage. I did not want to expose myself to another such life-altering episode. However, as I witnessed Debra's desire to mother a child, I gave in to her strong desire to become a mother. Our son, Justin, was born on June 1, 1982. I now realize that agreeing to have another child was one of the best decisions I have ever made. On second thought, it was the very best decision.

As a widower with self-imposed minimal socialization, I cannot imagine my life without Justin and his family, especially my grandson Asher, who just celebrated his six-month birthday. The joy that little guy brings into my life is indescribable, and it is so comforting to know that Debra's legacy lives on through our son and grandson.

LESSON LEARNED

Life can be unpredictable, and we should cherish and find time to be with those we love as often as possible.

FINITO

Now approaching the age of 90, I find that I am in reasonably good health for a person my age. I have lived a long and eventful life, but it has not been without its share of tragedy, especially in losing many family members and friends. I have outlived two wives, three of my four siblings, and two children, all younger than me. I have also survived several of my close, personal friends, many of whom date back to my youth.

Despite my many challenges, I have always tried to remain optimistic and appreciate the blessings in my life. However, as I now embrace the purported "Golden Years" of my life, I often feel that my long life is a blessing and a burden.

My siblings and one of my children died of common diseases, with a daughter whose life was taken by another. My first wife, Judy, passed away of natural causes at the age of 84, and even though we had divorced nearly 50 years before her death, we maintained a friendly concern and respect for each other until her end. My second wife, Debra, was 18 years my junior but lost her brave battle with cancer at 69. I now, by self-design, live mostly in solitude. I carry on, finding comfort in memories of those whom I loved but have departed life here on earth. I also find much solace in the love I experience from those of my remaining family.

Over the years, I sadly watched as my siblings and children passed away individually. Each loss was a heartbreak, and I have often questioned why I have been spared while those I loved have been taken.

I have made good friends over the years and have become noted as someone who can be relied upon to help others, expecting nothing in return willingly. I am proud to have been noted for my resilience and unwavering optimism, with some turning to me for guidance and support.

But as I prepare to enter what will probably be the last decade of my life, I have begun to feel the weight of my long life. I have grown tired of watching my loved ones pass away before me, and I sometimes feel lonely and isolated. My body is beginning to fail me, and I find myself struggling with daily tasks that had once been quite simple.

I realize I am fortunate to have lived such a long and full life, but as I mentioned, I also feel that my longevity is a burden. I sometimes long for the peace and rest that I hope awaits me in the afterlife, but I also question, with a certain amount of anxiety, what lies beyond. I cherish the memories of my loved ones and the good times we shared, but I also feel a deep sense of loss and grief.

Sitting at the computer composing this book's final story of my long life, I reflect on my life and all I have experienced. I know that my time on this earth is ending, but I also know that I have been blessed with a long and fulfilling life.

So, after nearly a decade of writing, with my fingers waiting now on the keyboard, I strike the last letter of the word "finite" and take a long perspective sigh of accomplishment. With a feeling of gratefulness for the time I have been given, I now prepare to face whatever lies ahead.

LESSON LEARNED

We, as mere humans, are not in control of our lives and the lives of those we love. That control is in the hands of a higher power, who or what that may be.

AFTERWORD

As we close the final pages of this remarkable journey through the tapestry of the author's life, we are left with a profound sense of gratitude and reflection. In sharing his life's stories – a mosaic of triumphs and tribulations – the author has gifted us with tales and a compass for navigating the complexities of our own lives.

Each story, a snapshot of a moment in time, carries a lesson hard-earned and generously imparted. From the exhilarating peaks of joy and success to the valleys of despair and loss, the author's candid recounting reminds us that life is not a linear path but a series of undulating experiences that shape who we are.

This collection is particularly striking because of the author's resilience and optimism. Even in the most trying times, he finds a kernel of wisdom, a lesson to be learned, a reason to move forward with hope. This perspective is a powerful reminder that our attitude and reactions to life's events can be our most potent tools.

His stories also underscore the importance of mindfulness and gratitude. In his reflections, the author often finds joy in the simplest moments – a testament to the richness of life when we are fully present and appreciative of our experiences.

This book is more than a memoir; it's a guide. It encourages us to examine the events of our lives, find our lessons, and share them. It inspires us to live more fully, to embrace life with all its unpredictability, and to find joy and purpose in every step of the journey.

As we put this book down, we carry with us the wisdom of a well-lived life that faced challenges head-on and celebrated its victories with humility and grace. May these stories serve as a beacon, guiding us toward a more joyful, purposeful, and reflective life.

In sharing his life, the author has not only chronicled his journey but has also illuminated ours. For that, we are immeasurably grateful.

ABOUT THE AUTHOR

Born in 1935, the author's beginnings were humble. He grew up on a farm in Southwest Missouri in a home without electricity, running water, a telephone, or indoor plumbing. From those beginnings, Smith received his bachelor's degree in speech and drama from the University of Missouri. After a career as a disc jockey and a move to Los Angeles, he worked as a copywriter at a local individually-owned advertising agency. After eight years with the agency and promotions leading to vice president, Smith left to open his advertising agency in 1972. From a one-man operation, Smith built his regional agency into a 25-person shop with billings above $5 million and a roster of marque clients, including In-N-Out Burger and Postal Instant Press.

In the mid-1980s, Smith closed his agency and retired to Palm Springs, California. Quickly learning that retirement didn't agree with his penchant for achievement, Smith then created and launched a local television golf program, *T-Time, with Tommy Jacobs*. The program aired daily on a local Palm Springs area cable TV channel for ten years. In 2008, Smith and his wife, Debra, pulled up stakes and moved to the Boston area to be close to their son, Justin, after he was accepted to Harvard University. While in Boston, Smith again became bored and returned to school at Northeastern University, where he graduated summa cum laude in 2011 with a master's degree in leadership. He continued his studies and completed all courses for a doctoral degree in 2013. He chose "An Assessment of Storytelling as a Leadership Skill" as the subject for his dissertation. However, he did not complete a dissertation, making him ABD (All But Dissertation).

Now an Austin, Texas resident, Smith is keenly interested in leadership storytelling. While he observes it evolving commercially, he maintains it is absent from most higher education leadership course curricula. So, instead of further pursuing his passion for seeing more universities and colleges teach storytelling,

Smith wrote a book about the personal stories of his own life, *The Seasons of a Storied Life.*

PARTING THOUGHTS BY THE AUTHOR

My adult life has been an economic and emotional roller coaster…with some very enjoyable highs and some very miserable lows. Through it all, I have found a way to survive and see, now in the octogenarian decade of my life, that I have accumulated many short stories, all of which have affected my life – some in desirable ways and others in less-than-desirable ways. Reflecting upon these life stories, I conclude that each has taught me a lesson. So, I committed myself to completing this book with the intent that by telling them, others may benefit and learn important lessons from my stories.

Without forethought or intent, the number of stories in my book totals sixty-six. While I am not immersed in numerology, I was curious about any significant meaning of 66. So, I did some research, and here are my findings.

When angel number 66 appears in your life, it carries a message from your angels about abundance, optimism, and creativity. Whenever your angels communicate using a repeating number or group of digits, the repetition is meant to provide emphasis and power to their message. Number 66 is a powerful message about love and healing.

Made in the USA
Columbia, SC
04 July 2024

589674ed-ca03-43a3-bebf-2d0fa3dae2b5R01